W9-CHR-447

Revised Edition

Great Quarterbacks #2

KILMER · BRADSHAW
HADL   PHIPPS

Bill Gutman

tempo books

GROSSET & DUNLAP
Publishers   New York

ISBN: 0-448-07429-X

Revised and updated from Great Quarterbacks #2

Tempo Books is Registered in the U.S. Patent Office
A Tempo Books Original
Published Simultaneously in Canada

Printed in the United States of America

To Frank Yohan,
a number one football fan
and number one guy

ACKNOWLEDGMENTS

The author wishes to thank the following people for their help in supplying background material for this book: Joe Browne and Kay O'Reilly of the National Football League office; the publicity departments of the Washington Redskins, Pittsburgh Steelers, San Diego Chargers, Los Angeles Rams, and Cleveland Browns; Keith Prince, Sports Information Director at Louisiana Polytechnic Institute; and the sports information departments at UCLA, and the University of Kansas. Thanks also to Ted Haracz of Purdue University, who has helped with past projects as well as this one.

CONTENTS

BILLY KILMER

Bill Kilmer has always had a reputation as a certain kind of guy. His guts and determination have been admired and respected for a long time, even before he attained his current star status with the Washington Redskins.

One of the greatest of all professional quarterbacks, Bart Starr, used to tell a story on the banquet circuit whenever someone asked him how he became the Packer quarterback. The tale really had no connection with Kilmer, that is, until a former pro football coach heard it one night. It went something like this:

"When Coach Lombardi came to Green Bay the first thing he did was build a large brick wall at the end of the field. Then he told all the players to run toward it full tilt. The ones who banged into it and fell backwards became defensive lineman. Those who

cracked into it and fell on their stomachs became offensive linemen. The ones who ran through it were
the fullbacks, and the ones who ran up to the wall,
stopped, then walked around it became quarterbacks."

After hearing this story one night, the former coach
grinned and remarked, "Lombardi would have been
thoroughly confused if he sent Billy Kilmer at that
wall. Billy would run into it, run through it, jump
over it, or walk around it ... anything that it took to
win. Lombardi wouldn't have known where to play
him."

Vince Lombardi never coached Billy Kilmer. If he
had, however, he would have known exactly where to
play him. For one way or another, Billy Kilmer is a
quarterback. He may defy convention; he may not
have the natural physical attributes; he may do things
his own way—but Kilmer is all quarterback.

Washington Redskin tight end, Jerry Smith, no little guy himself, once looked at a bruised and battered
Kilmer coming into the locker room after a game and
said, "If it was three o'clock in the morning and I had
to go down a dark alley, I'd want him with me."

That kind of respect doesn't come easy, but
William Orland Kilmer earned it, and he didn't do it
the easy way. After all, it's not many quarterbacks
who are told:

They may not live.

They may lose a leg.

They will never play football again.

And it isn't every quarterback who can sit on a professional bench for the better part of three seasons

seeing less action then the water boy, then bounce back with a display of skills people never knew existed. But Billy Kilmer did it.

On December 24, 1972, an overflow crowd gathered in Washington's Robert F. Kennedy Stadium to watch their beloved Redskins do battle with the Green Bay Packers in the first round of the National Conference playoffs.

The hometown fans hooted and cheered as each Redskin starter was introduced and trotted onto the field. But they saved the longest and loudest cheers for number 17, their quarterback, a 33-year-old veteran named Billy Kilmer.

Fans watching Kilmer jog confidently onto the field and begin exhorting his teammates with shouts and smacks on the back wouldn't have known it was the same man who, exactly 10 years earlier, lay flat on his back in a San Francisco hospital fighting for his life, his leg, and his professional career. Lombardi's brick wall would have looked awfully big to him then.

Kilmer had come to the Skins in 1971, in the first of many trades engineered by new head coach George Allen. After struggling at San Francisco and taking his lumps with expansionist New Orleans, Kilmer should have been happy going to the rebuilding Redskins. But he wasn't, and that was because the Washington team had a quarterback named Sonny Jurgensen, widely regarded as one of the best passers ever. The thought of once again being a backup didn't appeal to this competitive fireball from Topeka, Kansas.

But Allen knew what he wanted. When someone questioned the trade, the coach snapped, "Kilmer is a fighter. He never quits. He's done a tremendous job at New Orleans. He's the kind of competitor and leader I want around here. No matter where I was coaching I'd want him. He'll be ready whenever we need him."

The need came. An injury to Jurgensen in the exhibition season made Kilmer number one for the entire 1971 season. And what did he do? He led the Washington Redskins to their best record in 29 years and into the NFL playoffs. Like the man said, when they needed him, Billy Kilmer was ready.

There was a time when William Orland Kilmer wasn't ready. It was by no fault of his, however. Bad luck seemed to dog the gritty quarterback from the beginning of his career.

Not from the beginning of his life, though. That was a happy time. Billy was born in Topeka on September 5, 1939. When he was just a youngster his parents moved to California where his father, Orland Kilmer, opened a dry cleaning business. Mr. Kilmer was away from home some 10 to 12 hours a day, and when young Bill saw his first football game it was with his grandfather at the Los Angeles Coliseum.

"I guess I was about five then," Bill recalls. "I know that my feet wouldn't even reach the floor when I sat in the chair. Anyway, my grandfather took me to the game and I can remember sitting in the crowded stands and thinking even then that I wanted to be just like those football players on the field. It just looked so great to be playing in front of so many people. I told my grandfather that I wanted to be a football player when I grew up. I don't know if he believed me, but we were always great pals and he took me to a game almost every week."

Grandpa Kilmer wasn't the only member of the family to encourage young Bill in athletics. His mother had once pitched on a ladies softball team that won the Women's World Series at Soldier Field in Chicago, and she still got a kick out of pitching the ball to her son in the backyard of their home. So that took care of football and baseball.

Orland Kilmer handled the basketball end of it. He put up a board and hoop in the yard and Billy used to shoot at it for hours on end.

"It was a great way to relieve my frustrations," said Billy. "Whenever I wanted to think about something or make some plans, I'd go out and shoot baskets. That's when I got my ideas."

And that wasn't all. Mr. Kilmer had been Missouri Valley Swimming champion and once had an opportunity to try out for the Olympic team. As a result, swimming came easily to Bill and he could hold his own in the water with anyone.

When he got to junior high school he began putting his all-around athletic skills to work and he quickly found out something about himself.

"I loved competition," Bill recalls, "right from the first. It was the challenge to win. I always wanted to be the very best at everything I did."

When Billy arrived at Azusa High School, he was a multi-sport star, a performer for all seasons who electrified the Azusa fans with his exploits on the playing fields. At first, the six-foot, 190-pound Kilmer preferred basketball. He liked the constant movement and hectic non-stop action of the court game. He was a standout at guard, ball-handling, driving, and jump-shooting with the best of them. He led the Azusa team to a near-perfect record for three seasons. The team lost just one league game in that time and Kilmer became Southern California scoring champion, pumping nearly 2,000 points through the hoop in three seasons.

But he didn't neglect the other sports. He may not have liked baseball as much, but he played the game with consummate skill. In fact, by the time he was a senior the scouts were coming around in droves and the word on Kilmer was out. There was talk of a $50,-000 bonus with the Pirates, and Billy liked the sound of that.

"I was all set to sign and leave for training camp," he revealed, "but my mother intervened. She was determined that I go to college and my father agreed. Then I thought it out and decided it was the right thing.

"Besides, by then I was really in love with football. That's why I chose UCLA. They still played the single wing formation and I wanted a chance to be a tailback. I wanted to be a triple-threat man—running, passing, and kicking. There weren't too many of those guys left anymore."

So, after a year at Citrus Junior College, Billy went to UCLA with the prime objective of playing tailback. But what is a tailback? You don't really hear the term much anymore.

That's because the single wing as an offensive formation is almost completely gone today. All schools use the standard "T," the pro set, the wishbone-T, or some other variation. But in each of these cases, the play is started by the quarterback taking a direct snap from the center.

With the single wing, the quarterback was merely a blocking back, standing to the right or left of center and calling signals. He rarely touched the ball on offense. The focal point of the attack was the tailback, who stood about five yards behind the center and took a direct snap. From there, the tailback would either run, throw, or kick when necessary. Occasionally, he'd hand the ball to his fullback, who stood in the backfield with him. But more than 90 percent of the time, the tailback started the play.

When Kilmer arrived at UCLA, there were still a handful of college teams using the single wing. The UClans were among them, and there Bill could realize his long-standing dream of playing tailback. Coach George Dickerson knew the multi-talented halfback from Azusa could do it all, and immediately installed him as a tailback candidate during his sophomore year of 1958.

By the end of the practice season, Bill had won the starting tailback job and opened the season against the University of Pittsburgh. It looked as if his dream was about to come true. On the first series of downs, Bill began marching the Bruins downfield. With the ball on the 40, he took a direct snap, dropped back another two or three yards, then heaved a long pass to his flanker back. The receiver gathered it in at the goal line and went over for a score.

Billy came to the sidelines, the cheers of the crowd

ringing like music in his ears. He was proud and
happy, and thought back to the days when his grandfather used to take him to the games. His grandfather
and the rest of his family were in the stands that day
and it made Billy even happier.

The UClans eventually lost that one, 27-6, but Kilmer had shown enough to win the regular tailback
job. The rest of the team was young and inexperienced, but Billy was happy to be in there. He had a
fine second game, helping defeat Illinois, 18-14, and
with a win under his belt, looked forward to meeting
another single win team, Oregon State, the next week.

Then, early in the game it happened. There was a
pileup on a running play and Bill got up holding his
right hand. Someone had stepped on it and he left
the game. X-rays showed a broken bone and he was
out. Terribly disappointed, the combative Kilmer had
to sit the bench until the final game. Against USC he
saw limited action, played well, and was instrumental
in helping his team to a 15-15 deadlock.

Bill was happy to be back, but he was also thinking
of the next season and a chance to redeem himself for
what he considered a lost year. There were those who
agreed with him; a local paper said, "Nothing is
going to stop Billy Kilmer next year."

With a new coach in Bill Barnes and a more ex-
perienced team, the Bruins looked to a big year.
Barnes was counting on Kilmer as his starting tailback.
Then fate took a hand once again.

Umpiring an intramural baseball game, Bill was
struck on his ankle by a foul ball. The ankle wasn't
broken, but bruised severely enough to shelve him

once again. This time he couldn't run, and by the time the season was almost over, he was out of shape and overweight. He struggled to get ready, and with the ankle still tender, managed to get into the last five games.

He saw some action against Stanford and North Carolina State, then came back against unbeaten USC. Playing in sneakers because his ankle was too sore for football cleats, the gutty Kilmer hobbled through a few running plays. But mostly he passed—and he was on target. When the day ended, the Bruins were 10-3 winners, and Kilmer shared the glory with the UCLA defense, which had bottled up the Trojan attack most of the afternoon.

Bill did the same thing the following two weeks, helping to defeat Utah, 21-6, then participating in a losing effort against Syracuse, 36-8. But the club had improved and managed a 5-4-1 record with everyone looking forward to the 1960 season. One writer, however, voiced cautious optimism, something everyone felt.

"For two seasons now," he wrote, "the Bruins have had a potentially outstanding tailback in young Bill Kilmer. When he's right, the experts say he's at least the equal of Paul Cameron, Primo Villanueva, Sam Brown, and Ronnie Knox, the top tailbacks since the Bruins began using the single wing a dozen years ago.

"But Kilmer has never had a chance to really show his stuff. The injury jinx has hit this youngster from Azusa, and hit him hard. A broken hand and severely bruised ankle have cost him the better part of two seasons. Now, as a senior, he has one last chance to show that he rates with the best. Let's hope he stays healthy . . . for everyone's sake."

He stayed healthy. It took a few games for him to get the feel of being a fulltime tailback, and the defense had to mature, too, but the Bruins soon showed signs of being one of the best teams in the country, with Kilmer the spiritual and physical leader.

UCLA opened with an 8-7 win over Pittsburgh, then tied Purdue at 27-all. A 10-8 loss to Washington followed, so the team was 1-1-1 after three games. But Kilmer was already making his mark. He fired three TD passes in the deadlock with Purdue, and according to most observers, outplayed Washington QB Bob Schloredt even though the Bruins lost.

After a 26-8 victory over Stanford, the Bruins edged North Carolina State, 7-0, as Billy outplayed State's Roman Gabriel, considered by many as the best T-quarterback in the country. Two big victories followed that, a 28-0 win over California, and a 22-0 whitewash of the Air Force Academy. And suddenly Kilmer was attracting national attention.

Though statistics are not really a true measure of a player's worth, in Bill's case they helped. Because his combined running and passing yardage put him near the top of the pack in the race for national total offense leader. A healthy Kilmer was proving the experts right. He was one of the best.

A loss to arch-rival USC followed, but Kilmer and the Bruins then closed out the year with wins over Utah and Duke. The team was 7-2-1 for the season and Kilmer had taken the total offense title.

Playing in all 10 Bruin games, Billy had carried the ball 163 times for 803 yards, averaging nearly five yards a carry. In addition, he completed 64 of 129 passes for 1,086 yards and eight touchdowns. His total was 1,889 yards, and he took the total offense crown by more than 150 yards. He completed his dream of being a triple-threat star by punting for a 42.3 yard average on 35 kicks, and that was good for fifth best in the entire country.

And he got more recognition than that. Coach Barnes called him the best tailback UCLA ever had. He was named to the Football Writers' Association and *Sporting News* All-America teams. On four occasions he was Southern California Player of the Week, and five times he was named Big Five Back of the Week. But it wasn't only on the coast. He was a two-time Associated Press National Back of the Week and twice a member of the UPI Backfield of the Week. It was quite a year, and the end of an era as well. Kilmer was the last great single wing tailback at UCLA. Soon after he left the UClans switched to the straight-T formation, as most colleges were changing their style of play.

What to do now? After all, the pros didn't play the single wing. It was the straight T all the way in the NFL. There was a time when Bill planned to go into the dry cleaning business with his father, but now football was in his blood. He had to give it a try. He was married by then, and had an infant daughter. He worried about his wife and child, but since he had the family business to fall back upon, nothing would be lost if football didn't work out.

The main problem was finding a position. He knew he could run the ball and he knew he could throw. But could he do either well enough to play halfback or quarterback in the pros? Many of the scouting reports read: Too slow to be a halfback; not a strong enough arm to be a quarterback. It looked like a dead end.

There were other T-quarterbacks that year, men like Fran Tarkenton and Norman Snead, and they were grabbed right away by the pros. Kilmer figured he'd have to wait. But then he heard the news. The San Francisco 49ers, a better-than-average club, picked him as their first draft choice.

Billy couldn't believe it. He knew that the 49ers had two fine quarterbacks in veteran Y. A. Tittle and young John Brodie. They also seemed set at halfback. He wondered just what they had planned for him.

It didn't take him long to find out. San Francisco coach Red Hickey called on Billy and explained what he had in mind. Hickey thought football was ready for a change. He planned to open the 1961 season with a new offensive formation. It was tabbed the "Shotgun," and would feature the quarterback taking a direct snap from center.

"You mean it's similar to the single wing?" an astonished Billy asked.

"Similar," said Hickey, "in that I'll need a quarterback who can run as well as pass."

"I'm your man," said Billy. And suddenly he had a new lease on life.

The shotgun wasn't a new formation. It was similar to the old double-wing, giving the offensive team an extra wide receiver. The immortal Glenn "Pop" Warner had used it at Stanford right after World War I, and several other colleges had used it on occasion. It was known as a potent passing formation, the theory being that the passer didn't have to turn his back on the field as the T-quarterback often does while retreating. The shotgun passer could watch his receivers throughout the entire pattern.

Of course, he didn't have as many options on running plays. That's why the shotgun triggerman (you couldn't really call him a quarterback) had to be able to lug leather himself. Put those prerequisities into the 1960 collegiate hopper and the answer came out K-I-L-M-E-R.

The situation with the 49ers was strangely parallel to something that had happened some 20 years earlier. The year was 1940 and Stanford University was using the double-wing formation. There was a 175 pound kid named Frankie Albert on the squad. Since he was so small they didn't know what to do with him. Then new coach Clark Shaughnessy decided to switch to the T. In Albert, he found a perfect quarterback.

Frankie went on to the 49ers and a great career as a lefthanded passer in the National Football League. The T had saved Albert's career, and now it looked as if the shotgun might save Kilmer's.

Billy was excited about beginning his professional career. But he had a stop to make first. Because of his all-around ability he was chosen to play in the annual College All-Star Game in Chicago, with the top collegians going against the world champion Philadelphia Eagles. At practice, Kilmer so impressed Coach Otto Graham that he installed Billy behind Norman Snead at the quarterback position, the T-quarterback position.

Philadelphia quickly took a lead, pushing around the inexperienced collegians without much trouble. It soon became evident that Snead couldn't move the All-Stars. Graham knew he had to shake up his team so he replaced the classic passer with the street fighter. Billy Kilmer went into the game.

Suddenly the stars seemed to come to life. With Kilmer handing the ball off, carrying it himself, and throwing, they began to move. Three times they drove upfield. The first two times the Eagle defense stiffened and held. The third time they couldn't stop Kilmer. He passed for first downs on three consecutive plays as the huge crowd roared. The Stars jumped to the line breathing fire. Kilmer barked signals, took the snap, and ran straight up the middle through the heart of the Philly defense, picking up 13 yards and another first down.

Like most great players, Kilmer is an opportunist. He knew the Eagles were down and he wanted to strike fast. He took the snap and dropped straight back. Playing the unfamiliar T didn't seem to bother him at all. He looked downfield and rifled a pass to Glynn Gregory in the end zone. Touchdown! Kilmer had thrown for a 17-yard score and the Stars were on the board.

His leadership continued throughout the rest of the game, and he drove his team to another late score. The final was 28-14 in favor of the Eagles, but Kilmer was the talk of the town. He was voted the Most Valuable All-Star Performer, something very few people would have bet on before the game began. But Billy was never one to rest on his laurels. After the game he headed right for the 49er camp, ready to start all over again.

When he got there he found that Coach Hickey was indeed working hard at the new shotgun formation. He had already made one move, deciding that the veteran Tittle was too old and slow to trigger the shotgun, so he traded the old quarterback to the New York Giants. The other triggermen were Brodie, essentially a passer, and a rookie named Bobby Waters, whose forte was running the ball. Kilmer, it seemed, offered the best pass-run combination of the three.

Very few quarterbacks in the NFL camp step in and do a job from day one. It takes several years for the T quarterback to learn all the intricacies of his trade. Some never learn. But when Billy lined up in the shotgun for the first time he felt right at home. The players were bigger, faster, and stronger, but otherwise he could have sworn it was UCLA all over again.

"Since I was a single-wing tailback in college," Bill said, "this is the only possible formation that I could step into without a long period of training."

Before long, the roles of the three rotating quarterbacks became obvious. Brodie was a professional thrower all right, by far the best pure passer in the group. But he wasn't a runner of any sort. He could scamper for shelter when pursued, but couldn't do much on designed running plays. Waters, on the other hand, was quite a fine runner who might have had a shot at a halfback job. But his passing left something to be desired and it was a risk any time he threw the football.

Kilmer easily presented the best combination as triggerman. He wasn't a speed merchant and didn't have the fine moves of a Hugh McElhenny, but he knew how to run and he had guts. He'd gain yardage. And his passing was certainly above average. They said he didn't have the arm to be a pro quarterback, but he had shown more than adequate poise and passing in the All-Star game, and he was doing it again from the shotgun.

Brodie could pass; Waters could run—but it was Kilmer who moved the team.

San Francisco opened the season with a flourish as the shotgun put points on the scoreboard in bunches. And early in the season it became obvious that Kilmer was more or less the regular. Brodie came in on some passing situations, Waters when a fresh runner was needed. Kilmer himself ran much more often than he passed, but the threat of the pass was present on every play and that made him more effective.

The team was in the running during the early part of the year, but after the halfway point, some of the other clubs began to catch up with the shotgun. Most observers figured the newness of the formation accounted for its effectiveness in the early going.

"What did you expect," wrote one newsman. "Most teams work at defensing the T. That's what they see, week after week. Suddenly, along comes the shotgun and takes them by surprise. But give them a few weeks to study it, learn what makes it tick, and they'll be ready, even the teams that haven't seen it before. That's what makes these guys pros."

But while there was now some doubt about the ultimate success of the formation, there was no doubt about Bill Kilmer's ability to run it. Just past the mid-season mark, league statistics showed that Billy was number six in the league rushing race.

"Pro football hasn't been easy for me," said the flashy rookie. "I've learned more here already than I did in my entire career before this. But with Coach Hickey calling the plays, I can concentrate strictly on execution and I think that's helped."

Someone asked Billy if he didn't think the shotgun was too predictable since he ran so much more than he passed.

"I'm not sure about that. We'll have to see. But I'll tell you one thing. I threw the ball more often than a T-quarterback runs. So the defense has to be ready for both."

The last few weeks of the season were tough ones. The offense wasn't moving nearly as well as it had earlier and many were beginning to think the shotgun had run its course. The team finished with a mediocre 7-6-1 record, winding up fifth in the Western Conference of the NFL. What had been a season of great expectations turned into a disappointment.

Though one scribe called Bill "the first quarterback since Sammy Baugh to attain instant stardom," there were some low points. First of all, the team didn't win. And winning always meant everything to Billy. And secondly, he wondered if he could accurately be called a quarterback. With the future of the shotgun in doubt, he could easily become a player without a position.

Statistically, he had an outstanding year. He had carried the ball 96 times, gaining 509 yards on an average of 5.3 yards per carry. And he was the bread-and-butter man around the goal line, scoring 10 touchdowns, including a record four in one game against the Vikings.

In the passing department, he really didn't have the chance to prove much, throwing just 34 times and completing 19 for 286 yards. Some quarterbacks do as much in a single game.

Tight end Mike Ditka of the Chicago Bears was the Rookie of the Year that season, and Bill couldn't even claim to be the best rookie quarterback. Fran Tarkenton, the freshman signal-caller of the Vikings, passed for almost 2,000 yards, and 18 touchdowns, and scrambled for 308 on the ground. When they met head to head, Kilmer helped San Francisco produce two victories, 38-24, and 38-28.

Yet Billy must have wondered what the future held. He was somewhat in limbo and wanted a chance to prove himself again. He'd have to, especially if the shotgun was abandoned.

It wasn't. Hickey wanted to give it one more try in 1962, and Billy again figured large in his plans. The young tailgunner went into the new year full of optimism, but before long he realized that it was just more of the same. In fact, it was worse. The team wasn't putting nearly as many points on the board, and it was giving up more. They weren't winning, and it was becoming obvious that the shotgun was slowly grinding to a halt.

Billy was the same kind of player in 1962. He ran much more often than he passed, and ran effectively. On the rare occasions that he did throw, his passes were wobbly, but accurate.

By the time the club had completed its first 12 games, Bill's stats were comparable to those of his rookie season. He had rushed 93 times for 478 yards and a 5.1 average, scoring five touchdowns along the way. Passing, he was just eight of 13 for 191 yards, but that was good for another score. Although there were still two games left, it was apparent that the 49er were not going to play .500 ball. (They finished at 6-8.)

Billy Kilmer didn't play in those final two games. In fact, for a long while it looked as if he had played his last football game ever. Bill didn't know it when he finished practice the afternoon of December 5, 1962, but he was about to embark on the biggest battle of his young life.

He left camp and began driving to the city on the Bayshore Freeway. Bill was a tired man. The team had a couple of days off before the practice and he had been on a quick hunting trip. He was drowsy as he whipped the auto along the freeway at a fast clip. It's not clear just what happened next. A car might have veered into his path, or he might have fallen asleep, but in a flash, Kilmer's car was off the road and careening down a steep embankment.

The car rolled some 435 feet through a field and into a deep ditch. In the car lay an unconscious Bill

Kilmer, with a right leg badly fractured above the ankle, a severely slashed chin, and a deep gash over his right eye. He was also suffering from concussion and shock.

When rescue workers arrived, they had to use a crowbar and torch to get Kilmer out of the car. In that time muddy water from the ditch had seeped into the auto and was already causing infection in the leg. It was a nightmare.

"I'm sure I fell asleep at the wheel," Billy recalled later. "The car went off the road and began plunging into the ditch. I remember waking up as I went off. I knew if I let go of the wheel I'd be thrown out, so I held on. I figured if I went flying out anything could happen. Anyway, my right leg got caught under the brake pedal. I could feel it snap, and I could see the bone coming through."

When the doctors first examined him they weren't sure whether they could save the leg. They set the bones, and there was no real ligament damage. But the muddy water had started an infection. If it couldn't be controlled, the situation would be crucial.

Billy lay in the hospital bed for the next few days thinking about just one thing. Then he started asking questions. First he asked about the leg. They told him they could save it unless there were more complications. Then he asked about walking. They told him he'd probably never walk normally again. Finally, he asked the big one. He wanted to know if he'd ever play football again. The doctors said there was no chance.

"We'll see about that," Billy Kilmer said to himself.

The hospital stay extended to three months as the leg slowly healed and the danger of more infection ebbed. Billy just lay there all those days and not a minute passed in which he didn't think about football, about how much he wanted to play again.

"My dad came in one day and asked me what I planned to do with myself now," he recalls. "I knew, but I didn't tell him. He suggested I come into the dry cleaning business since I always said I would someday. I agreed to work with him, but I was already making plans to rehabilitate the leg."

Billy began hobbling around his father's store. Within three weeks he was doubly convinced that he had to play ball again. But he faced another operation on the leg the following June, this one to remove some floating bone chips that had accumulated. Then the doctor's work would be done. The rest was up to Bill.

He knew there was no chance to play in 1963, and he wasn't even listed on the 49er roster. The team slipped all the way to the bottom of the loop that year as Red Hickey and the shotgun offense were both booted out the door. But Bill couldn't think about that now. His first job was to get himself back into playing shape. He'd worry about a position later.

"I had to look at it that way," he explained. "My life was athletics and I figured I was too young to give it all up. I tend to get a little stubborn, especially about things I really want ... and this was something I really wanted. Nobody ever came out and said I *couldn't* play football any more. They just said they didn't think I would. Well, I had to find out for myself whether I could or I couldn't."

Bill worked out during 1963 and the early part of '64, pushing himself continually and slowly, ever so slowly, regaining his mobility in the ankle. He knew he might not have as much speed as he once had, but he was prepared to use whatever was left.

Then in July of 1964 it became official. Billy was rejoining the squad and would be a full playing member when training camp opened the following week. The 49ers had a new coach by then, Jack Christiansen, who promptly returned the team to the more traditional T formation. John Brodie would be the quarterback, and a strong-armed youngster from Miami, George Mira, was slated to be the backup. That left Kilmer somewhere between third string and a halfback job.

San Francisco president Lou Spadia talked about Kilmer at a news conference. "The doctors say Billy is sound of limb," said Spadia. "If enthusiasm, courage, and guts can bring him all the way back, then I know he'll make it. In fact, he may be around for a long time."

As soon as camp opened, Christiansen made it known that Billy would be used as a running back only. Kilmer didn't complain. Making the team was his first goal.

In early August the team had its first all-out scrimmage at Kezar Stadium. When Billy entered the game, the fans who had come out to watch gave him a rousing reception. Buoyed by their cheers, the former shot-gun triggerman ran well and apparently without pain in his ankle. It was hard to believe. When the scrimmage ended he was the leading runner of the day with 37 yards on seven carries. And on one play he took a hand-off, faked an end sweep, and suddenly whipped a 13-yard TD pass to Monty Stickles. Kilmer could still hurt an opponent in more ways than one.

But the music just wasn't there. It was a matter of timing, a new position, and some faster, stronger backs ahead of him. Christiansen used him sparingly all season, though there were those who felt his leadership ability and inspirational play could have helped the team, especially since a 4-10 season kept the 49ers mired in the basement.

As it was, Billy carried just 36 times for 113 yards. As an option passer he was eight of 14 for 92 yards and a score. But it wasn't much of a season. And to add even more confusion to the situation, Christiansen approached him when it was all over and said he wanted him back as a quarterback in '65.

Billy jumped at the news. In his heart, this was what he wanted to do. But he realized it wouldn't be easy. Christiansen treated him like any other player and Bill knew he had to make the team on his own. He survived the final cut, but saw little action in the exhibition games. In the final pre-season game against the Rams he got in long enough to throw three passes. They were the last three he'd throw all year. Brodie and Mira were still ahead of him, and, to make matters worse, he reinjured the bad ankle. He didn't get in for one play.

By now, even a positive thinker like Bill was becoming discouraged. Going into the 1966 season he was 27 years old and felt that his career hadn't even begun. The years of shotgun seemed like a dream. Now he was a third-string quarterback and it seemed as if he'd always been one. But he wouldn't quit, and when 1966 rolled around he was right back in there plugging.

Before the season started, Coach Christiansen talked about Billy's drawbacks and attributes.

"Bill's been throwing better than ever before this year," the coach said. "He doesn't have the great speed, the quickness, or the straight overarm delivery, but he compensates for all that with a great feel for the game. He's as knowledgeable as they come and has the instinct of good quarterbacks who know when to let go of the ball.

"As a runner he has the same type of feeling and can get away and through holes that others can't. Billy loves the game and is in it from start to finish, even when he's sitting on the bench. I have no qualms whatsoever about using him."

He sounded like a coach who was planning to use his number three quarterback. Somehow, it never came about. The 49ers were a .500 team in '66, but Christiansen hoped to get them back in contention and he stuck with Brodie most of the way. If desire counted, Billy would have been in there every play.

By the time the final game rolled around, Bill Kilmer had seen a total of ten minutes and seven seconds playing time, appearing in just three ballgames. With the club going nowhere, some of the local sportswriters were getting restless.

One noted how Kilmer never left Christiansen's side during the ballgames, as he tried to get as close to the action as he could. The writer noted that "his (Kilmer's) burning desire to play, coupled with Christiansen's refusal to let him do so, except infrequently, made for a pathetic frustration."

And the same man added a sentiment shared by many Bill Kilmer fans. "This has been a horrible year for Billy Kilmer. Hopefully, it will be the last. Since they have so little use for him themselves, the 49ers should trade him. Kilmer has the ability to be a top hand for another club."

That's tremendous confidence in a man who hadn't even quarterbacked from the T formation for a full period in six seasons. But Billy Kilmer is the kind of guy people believe in. That became evident early in 1967. The National Football League was expanding once more and a new franchise was being added in New Orleans. As with all expansion teams the Saints, as they were called, wanted some solid veteran players around whom to build a respectable club.

Looking over the crop of back-up and veteran quarterbacks, the Saints quickly made their first choice. They picked Billy Kilmer.

There was no doubt about Bill's reaction. He was happy that he'd finally have a chance to play ball, even though the Saints were an expansion club, a place where the quarterback is often not much more than a glorified punching bag. But he was confident and defiant.

"I'm not afraid of being hit, so you won't find me looking for the ends, tackles, and linebackers when I drop back to pass. I'll be looking for my receivers. If you start worrying about the guys who are coming after you, then you might as well just run away and hide.

"This is the chance I've been waiting for. The 49ers used me in one exhibition game a year. They had no room for me and I wanted to go someplace where I could play. That's all I ever wanted, a fair opportunity."

There were others who expressed confidence in Kilmer, men who knew what the game was all about. One was Y. A. Tittle, himself traded by the 49ers when Kilmer and the shotgun came on the scene in 1961. Y. A. went on to set records and win championships with the New York Giants. By 1967, he was retired and a special quarterback consultant for the 49ers.

Speaking before a banquet audience in New Orleans, the old quarterback talked about the new Saints and about Billy Kilmer.

"I'm sure you're all going to be very pleased with Kilmer," Y. A. said. "He's the Bobby Layne type of quarterback not a picture passer, but Layne wasn't, either. All Layne did was beat you.

"Kilmer has a fine touch, is an outstanding leader and has an extraordinary knowledge of the game, more so than most quarterbacks. Kilmer played behind John Brodie and George Mira at San Francisco, but there were times when some of us thought that maybe our best quarterback was sitting on the bench.

"It won't surprise me to see Bill become an outstanding quarterback here. He has the potential. He's had it for a long time."

By the time the exhibition season started, the Saints had picked up another quarterback, Gary Cuozzo, who had been an impressive back-up to John Unitas at Baltimore. Cuozzo was a standard dropback passer with a good arm. The only question was could he stand the gaff of playing behind an expansionist line?

Saints coach Tom Fears decided to alternate the two quarterbacks in the exhibition season. In the first game against the Rams, Cuozzo started and Kilmer relieved. The Saints lost, but Billy was outstanding in defeat and Fears named him the starter against St. Louis the following week.

As a starter, Bill immediately got the team moving. The line fired out at the snap, and the backs hit the holes, taking Kilmer's crisp handoffs. He was a fine field leader and moved the team well. But it was his passing that surprised everyone. As Y. A. Tittle had said, his passes weren't pretty, but they were getting there and the Saints had a couple of receivers who could hold onto the ball.

On two occasions, his passes found their mark in the end zone for scores and the Saints had a surprising, 23-14, victory. This set the pattern for the remainder of the exhibition season. Kilmer started with the first unit, with Cuozzo relieving. It was becoming apparent that Billy was winning the number one job.

Two more surprise victories followed. Then the Saints came up against the 49ers—a game Billy had been looking to with anticipation. It was played at

Portland, Oregon, with many San Francisco fans on hand. Most of them remembered Kilmer well.

And if they didn't, he let them know who he was in a hurry. The first time the Saints had the ball they began moving. With veteran Jim Taylor at fullback, Kilmer had a professional ball carrier to work with. He mixed his running plays with short and swing passes to the sideline, and the 49er defenders seemed confused.

With the ball at the San Francisco 25, Kilmer faded back again. This time he spotted flanker Walt Roberts streaking for the end zone. He fired a wobbler, but as Roberts crossed the goal line the ball was waiting for him and he grabbed it for a score.

In the second quarter, Kilmer led two more drives. The first carried to the four. The 49ers packed in tight, expecting a running play. But Kilmer rolled right, then flipped a short pass to Taylor for another score. Later he called an end around to rookie John Gilliam who bolted in from five yards out.

When Billy gave way to Cuozzo in the second half, he had completed 13 of 19 passes for 126 yards and two scores. And he'd given the Saints a 21-3 lead. His ball-control game helped keep the pressure off the New Orleans defense, and when the club won, 24-10, much of the credit belonged to Billy Kilmer.

"Billy did one fine job for us," said Coach Fears. "It isn't easy to take a team in the first drive of the game, but he did it with a real professional effort."

As for Billy, he said simply, "I loved it. It was real sweet. But don't forget, they'll get a chance to even things up when we meet again in October." He wasn't about to say anything that would inflame the 49ers and give them something to shoot for later. In that way, Bill was smart, too.

By the end of the exhibition season, the experts couldn't believe their eyes. Bill Kilmer had led the expansionist Saints to five straight victories. In those games he had fired for nine touchdowns, six more than Cuozza. And with the possible exception of the veteran Jim Taylor (who had played his college ball at Louisiana State before starring with the Packers), Kilmer was the most popular player on the new team.

Fears had not yet named his starting quarterback, but most observers were rooting heavily for Kilmer.

"It's the feeling down here that Kilmer ignites the team when he gets into the game," wrote one newsman. "He's unorthodox and the players believe in him no matter what he tries. This is evident even in practice."

If the exhibition victories were a pipe dream, the regular season turned into a nightmare. Billy opened at quarterback and played steady ball. But the Saints as a whole were making too many mistakes, something not uncommon for new teams. When it really counted, they found victories hard to come by. Three games and three losses, and Billy suddenly found himself on the bench.

"It was hard to take," he confessed. "I knew I could move this type of team better than Gary (Cuozzo), but we were losing and the coach had to see what some of the other guys could do."

Sitting the bench was Bill Kilmer's idea of Hades. It ate him up inside. Cuozzo didn't fare much better and Fears began alternating his signal-callers much as he did in the exhibitions. In the final home game with Atlanta Billy came off the bench in the second half to rally his club to a 27-24 victory over the two-year-old Atlanta Falcons.

He got the starting call again in the final regular season game against the Redskins in Washington. With the pressure on, Billy responded, leading the team as he had in the preseason. He moved his runners well, mixed his plays, and tossed a pair of touchdown passes, one an 80-yarder to rookie Dan Abramowicz. The Saints won it, 30-14, and although he didn't know it at the ime, Billy Kilmer had won himself a regular job.

The Saints finished with a 3-11 mark, a realistic figure for a first-year club. As for Billy, he'd had more opportunity than ever before, connecting on 97 of 204 passes for 1,341 yards and six touchdowns. His passing percentage was low at 47.5, but considering the circumstances, no one complained. He also finished as the team's third leading rusher with 142 yards on 20 carries. That's an average of 7.1, although he was running mainly on scrambles and broken plays.

By the following summer, Fears made his decision. He shipped Cuozzo off to Minnesota and told Bill he'd be going with him at quarterback. It marked the first time in his career that Bill Kilmer came to camp knowing he had himself a steady job.

"It's a great feeling to know you've finally got it made," said Bill to reporters. "Because I've had the chance to throw more in the last years, my arm is stronger than ever. Now the receivers know my passes better. There's a certain oneness forming throughout the team.

"We're all aware of the second-year lull like Atlanta experienced (the Falcons went from 3-11 to 1-12-1), but I'd say it's possible for the Saints to win 10 games this season." As usual, Billy was the eternal optimist.

Dave Whitsell, a veteran defensive back who had come to the Saints from the Chicago Bears, was also pleased to see Kilmer tabbed number one, and he told why.

"If Bill Kilmer decided to jump off a building, everyone here would jump with him," Whitsell said. "That's the kind of leader he is.

"I really think he's arrived. In fact, he's just a step away from greatness. I think he'll be the next Bobby Layne. He's got everyone around here thinking like winners. Layne did that, too."

It may have sounded like a lot of talk about a player who hadn't done much on the field. But in an early scrimmage against the San Diego Chargers, Billy showed his critics with a 14-of-22 day, good for 274 yards and three touchdowns. There was no longer much doubt about his ability to handle the T.

Several weeks later the Saints hosted the powerful Cleveland Browns in an exhibition game held before 70,045 fans at the Sugar Bowl in New Orleans. Kilmer turned them on again, connecting on 20 of 33 passes for 261 yards and two scores as the Saints routed the Browns, 40-27.

It wasn't an easy year. There were high points in the regular season, too, but a young team cannot pick up experience overnight. The Saints rolled over the Browns in the 40-27 exhibition, but when it counted during the year, Cleveland prevailed twice, 24-10, and 34-17.

The Saints were in the Century Division of the Eastern Conference during 1968, and, along with Cleveland, were joined by the Cardinals and Steelers. They lost to the Cards twice, but beat the Steelers a pair and actually finished higher than Pittsburgh in the standings. It was a 4-9-1 year for Coach Fears' club.

Billy was good, but not great. He suffered a hairline fracture of the ankle midway through the campaign. He missed the better part of three games—most players would have missed half a season.

There were some heroics for the home fans, but some low moments, too, when the Saints' offensive line couldn't keep the opposition out of the backfield, or when one of Bill's passes was off the mark and intercepted. Yet he still compiled the busiest year of his career, throwing 315 times, completing 167 for 2,060 yards and 15 touchdowns. His passing percentage was over 50, at 53.0, and he was intercepted 17 times.

It's hard to say whether the Saints' fans and management expected miracles, but as Kilmer began leading the team through the 1969 season, a slow chorus of jeers began greeting the quarterback. The jeers increased at each home game. Fans began chanting for a little-known youngster named Edd Hargett, who had played his college ball at Texas A & M.

Yet Kilmer was in the midst of his finest season to date. True, there were some off days, but everyone has off days, and with a three-year-old franchise, it's bound to happen even more.

There was a bad game against Philadelphia in which Bill was yanked out in the middle. But the next week, he went wild against the St. Louis Cardinals. It seemed that every time he got the ball he threw for a touchdown. Cards' QB Charley Johnson was hot, too, and both clubs marched up and down the field all afternoon. When it ended, Kilmer and the Saints had come out on top.

Billy had thrown the ball 32 times, completing 22 for 345 yards and six touchdowns. Johnson also threw for six scores (a record for two quarterbacks in one game), but Billy got one on the ground, also, and his club won, 51-42. It was the Saints' first win of the year.

The victory augured well for the second half of the year, but Billy Kilmer would again have to call on all his courage and guts to continue leading the club.

In a game against his old teammates, the 49ers, Billy suffered a severely separated left shoulder. He led the Saints to another win, 43-38, but after the game the doctors gave him the bad news.

"You need an immediate operation or the injury could lead to a permanent deformity of the shoulder."

"Can I play with it?" Kilmer asked.

"Yes, it won't get worse. But you know the consequences if you delay surgery."

"I'll play," said Kilmer without a moment's hesitation. When you wait as long as Billy Kilmer to be number one, you don't think about consequences.

Doctor Kenneth Saer, the Saints' physician, explained the injury to reporters. "It was a complete separation," said Dr. Saer. "It was the type of injury that required immediate surgery or could produce a painful joint. Without an operation he will have a deformity. His left shoulder will drop down and the clavicle (collar bone) will stick up."

It didn't matter to Kilmer. He continued to play, despite the painful shoulder and equally painful jeering from the fans.

A few weeks later, Billy started against the Steelers. Pittsburgh went ahead, 14-0, and the fans began chanting, WE WANT HARGETTT! Fears paced the sideline, debating whether to make a change. Suddenly Bill got hot, hitting seven straight passes and culminating the drive with a touchdown strike to end, Ray Poage.

At the half, Billy had completed nine of 14 for 148 yards. But the patchwork offensive line had allowed him to be sacked five times for a loss of 56 yards. The Steelers still led at the outset of the fourth quarter, 24-27, and Fears finally sent Hargett into the game. The fickle fans went wild, cheering the youngster as Kilmer walked slowly and sadly to the sideline.

Hargett led a drive downfield. With the ball near the goal line, Kilmer suddenly reentered to a shower of catcalls. Hargett had been shaken up and they wanted Bill's experience near the goal line. Sure enough, he set up the tying score and later the winning field goal. At the end his stats read 15 of 28 for 219 yards. Not bad. Asked about being pulled and the subsequent boos he heard, Bill was slightly angered.

"It's the coach's decision as to who plays and who doesn't. I'm just happy I made a contribution. As for the booing, it doesn't bother me normally, but it did a bit today because I thought I did a pretty good job."

There were additional victories—over the Eagles (26-17), and New York Giants (25-24)—giving the Saints a 5-9 mark and continued improvement, but Billy began feeling his days were numbered.

Statisically, he had his best year, completing 193 of 360 for 2,532 yards and 20 big touchdowns. Yet when the 1970 season opened, he found himself a part-timer, alternating with Hargett. There was increasing talk that the Saints were anxious to draft Mississippi's all-American, Archie Manning, and they were playing as though they wanted that last pick. After three years of progress, the Saints plummeted to a 2-11-1 mark. Wholesale changes were in order.

Billy threw just 237 passes that year, with six touchdowns to his credit against 17 interceptions. The high point of the season came in early November when he led the club to a 19-17 upset of the Detroit Lions, passing to Al Dodd in the closing seconds to set up Tom Dempsey's record-setting 63-yard field goal. But soon after the year was out, word began spreading that Kilmer would be traded.

"I asked out," said Billy, "as soon as they grabbed Manning in the draft. Where to go was another problem. I knew I couldn't go to a team with a youth movement in progress. By the time they were contenders I'd be too old to play anymore. I wanted my chance with a winner, a team ready to make a move on the championship."

The Washington Redskins was not one of those teams. The Skins were perennial losers. They had hired the great Vince Lombardi in 1969 and his coaching expertise and leadership moved the club to a 7-5-2 season. But Lombardi's untimely death set the Skins back and they were 6-8 in 1970. It looked as if they were starting all over again.

Then the Redskin owners signed George Allen, the fine coach of the Rams. Newsmen asked Allen what his building program for the future would be.

"The future is now," he snapped in a now famous statement. "I plan to make changes in this club before the season starts. I want proven players and I'll trade draft choices to get them. No rookie is going to pick up experience at my expense."

Allen was true to his word. He was at the helm a little over two weeks when he made his first deal. He sent a second stringer named Tom Roussel to New Orleans in exchange for Billy Kilmer. Allen told the press that Kilmer was a gutty leader who never quit, the type of player he'd want no matter where he was coaching.

But wait a minute. Didn't the Redskins have a quarterback, a man named Christian Adolph "Sonny" Jurgensen? Right! And wasn't he regarded as one of the greatest passers who ever lived! Right again. While Kilmer was having his big year in 1969, all Jurgy was doing was completing 274 passes in 442 attempts for 3,102 yards, 22 touchdowns, and a completion percentage of 62.0. That's the kind of thrower Sonny was. But he was also 37 years old and Allen wanted insurance.

"I wasn't very happy about going to the Redskins," Kilmer confessed. "There was no way I could step in and beat out Sonny for the starting job. I couldn't see myself as a backup again, not at this point. A couple of years as a backup again and people would forget about me. I saw myself on this team, but with my chance—my real chance—never coming."

Bill's fears seemed justified, at least by Allen's other statements immediately following the trade.

"Sonny Jurgensen is still my quarterback," said the coach with finality. "This deal has nothing to do with Sonny's status here. We got Billy as a backup, a backup who could step in and do the job if he has to. When you get a guy like Kilmer it's better than having a draft pick."

Bill did a great deal of soul-searching during the off-season. But he had faith in Allen and there was just one way he could play it. When he reported to camp, he was in shape and ready to go.

During camp, reporters looked for an intense rivalry between the two quarterbacks, and some were surprised when they became fast, close friends. Both QB's looked good in camp, with some saying Kilmer had the edge in moving the team. Then before the first exhibition, Jurgy bruised a thumb and Kilmer started against the San Diego Chargers.

Bill was still learning a new system and didn't look good. The Chargers won the game and one George Allen streak was ended. His teams had never lost in the preseason. Jurgy was healed the next week and he saw most of the action in the ensuing games. When Kilmer did play, he continued to look nervous and unsure, and a familiar chorus of boos began cascading down from the upper reaches of Robert F. Kennedy Stadium in Washington.

Then in the second to last exhibition, the Skins were in Miami facing the Dolphins. Jurgy wasn't having a good game. In the third quarter he tossed one over the middle that was picked off by safety Dick Anderson. An angered Jurgy forgot about an unwritten rule that the quarterback protect himself. He tore after Anderson and blasted through several blockers to help with the tackle. When he got up he was in obvious pain.

Jurgy came slowly to the sideline, his left shoulder slumping lower than his right. A bone in the shoulder had been fractured. Sonny was through for at least eight weeks.

Suddenly and unexpectedly there was another quarterback in the game for Washington. The first time the Skins got the ball he dropped back and rifled a 47-yard scoring pass to Roy Jefferson. Miami won the game, but Bill Kilmer quickly showed his club he was ready to assume leadership.

"When I finished that game," Kilmer recalls, "George called me in just to tell me the job was mine. He wouldn't make any more moves. He also told me how much confidence he had in me. Here's my chance, I thought. Now there'd be no more talking or thinking. I just had to go out there and do it."

To the press, Bill confidently announced, "I can win and operate as efficiently as Sonny. If I didn't think that way I wouldn't be doing much good for the team."

Many observers agreed. Said one long-time Redskin booster. "Kilmer is perfectly suited for the Redskins. He'll win with them. He controls the game, but unlike Sonny, doesn't dominate it. He inspires. He relates. And he knows his limitations."

Through several other shrewd deals, Allen had given Kilmer a much-improved team with which to work. The offense was fine, with super-runner Larry Brown and rugged Charley Harraway. Charley Taylor, Roy Jefferson, and Jerry Smith formed a first-rate trio of pass catchers. Both lines and the defensive linebackers and secondary were bolstered by the acquisition of able veterans, some aging, but all experienced and all winners.

The 1971 season opened in St. Louis with the Redskins coming to town as decided underdogs. Billy was deluged with a host of questions, most of them asking how he was going to fill Sonny Jurgensen's shoes.

"I'm not here to fill anyone's shoes," he snapped. "I'm here to follow a game plan and bring us home a winner."

It was a rainy, muddy Sunday as the Skins went up against the Cards. With the slippery football a risk to handle, Bill played it smart, sticking with basic running plays and only throwing occasionally. But one of his passes was a 31-yard touchdown strike to Smith and the Skins went on to win 24-17. Allen said Bill called a "masterful" game and he exhorted the team to continue winning.

Critics said Bill threw just six passes and didn't really prove anything, so a week later he went out and shut some mouths. He did it at the expense of the

Giants, in one of the most brilliant passing days of his career. He connected on 23 of 32 attempts for 309 yards. Two of his tosses went for TD's, both to Charley Taylor, one covering 71 yards, the other, two yards. He did it long and he did it short, as the Skins won, 30-3.

Suddenly the booing stopped. When the team came home, Kilmer was treated like a long-lost native son, an instant hero. And he didn't let them down. The next week he engineered a brilliant, 20-16, upset of the champion Dallas Cowboys, uncorking a 50-yard scoring toss to Jefferson to break the back of a Dallas rally. With Kilmer at the helm, the Skins had become bonafide contenders.

He made it four in a row the next week, leading his club to a 22-13 win over Houston, and the following Sunday he did it again, spearheading a 20-0 white-wash of St. Louis. The Skins were 5-0 and Billy Kilmer was riding high. Things were going so well with the surprising Redskins that some suggested the team might not be as successful if Jurgensen were playing. But the first to come to Sonny's defense was Bill Kilmer. He'd been there before.

"I say that we'd be doing even better if Sonny were playing. He's a winner who happens to be a fine person and great quarterback."

When someone suggested that Bill was being too modest, he replied promptly. "I'll never get a big head. I know as well as anyone that this kind of success lasts only as long as you win. But I'll say this much. I've never had an offense like this before. It's sensational. Coach Allen is building a club with an amazing amount of spirit. I just love being part of it."

The bubble burst the next week as the Skins fell victim to the tough Kansas City Chiefs, 27-20. After a victory over New Orleans and a surprise 7-7 tie with Philadelphia, Allen's club lost two more to the Bears and Cowboys. The Dallas game ended 13-0, and Kilmer was getting down about his performance.

But the team pulled out just in time. They won two more and then traveled to Los Angeles to face the Rams. Early in the first quarter Kermit Alexander intercepted a Kilmer aerial and galloped 82 yards for a touchdown return that gave L.A. a 7-0 lead. Right there it looked as if Kilmer and the Skins would fold.

But a few minutes later Kilmer dropped back to pass, totally undaunted by the interception, and whipped a long one down the right sideline to Roy Jefferson. The ball was right on the button, and Jefferson gathered it in and continued on his way to a 70-yard touchdown.

Later in the period Kilmer connected with Clifton McNeil on a 32-yarder, and just before halftime he went for it on a fourth and one, in close, calling on Larry Brown who bulled over to give the Skins a 24-10 halftime lead.

Another TD strike to Jefferson highlighted the second half and when it ended the Redskins had won the game, 38-24. As for Kilmer, he had completed 14 of 19 passes for 246 yards and three touchdowns. Bill played down his performance, but the Associated Press thought enough of it to name him the Offensive Player of the Week.

Cleveland whipped the Skins the final week of the

season, but Washington surprised with a 9-4-1 record, the best in 29 years, and entered the playoffs by having the best second-place mark in the NFC. Dallas captured the divisional crown at 11-3.

The first playoff game with San Francisco was a complete disappointment. The Skins fought hard, but were outgunned in the final quarter and beaten, 24-20. It was a double disappointment to Kilmer; the 49ers had been his first team. But the defeat couldn't cloud the Skins' amazing season. Allen himself said, "It was Bill Kilmer who brought us to the playoffs."

And a Washington newsman put Kilmer's performance into an even better perspective.

"Billy Kilmer did his job with a consistency that no one could have possibly predicted. He beat teams with his arm, with his head, and with his guts. He used everything at his command. He played the 1971 season with the candor of a street fighter. He would not lose. He would have to be beaten."

Statistically, Billy completed 166 of 306 passes for 2,221 yards and a 54.2 percentage. He tossed for 13 touchdowns and had an equal number of passes picked off. His teammates voted him Most Valuable Redskin and he finished fourth in the balloting for NFL Player of the Year. He was third in passing among all NFC quarterbacks.

In late January of 1972, Billy Kilmer won another award. He was voted the Most Courageous Athlete of 1971 by the Philadelphia Sports Writers Association. Bill was cited for coming back from his serious leg injury suffered in the auto crash, then overcoming other serious injuries to get the Redskins into the playoffs.

In his acceptance speech, the emotional Kilmer expressed his gratitude, then said he was going to give the award to someone in his family who deserved it more—his 12-year-old daughter, Kathy.

Kathy Kilmer was born with cerebral palsy and disjointed hips, and the little girl had undergone a series of operations to help her walk. When Billy received the award Kathy was facing still another operation and he had her on his mind. He was well aware that there were some things in the world more difficult than facing mammoth onrushing linemen.

When Billy reported to camp for the 1972 season he still didn't have the secure feeling that many pro quarterbacks enjoy. He had finished a strong number one, but Sonny Jurgensen was back, recovered from his injury, in shape, and ready to battle for his old job. Allen stated publicly that he'd go with the quarterback who had brought the team to the playoffs, but Billy and everyone else knew that if Jurgy was right, he couldn't be denied indefinitely.

As for the competition, the two quarterbacks had only good things to say about each other.

"Billy's a fine quarterback," said Sonny. "He knows the position and he's a leader. We try to help each other and this competition can only make us better."

Kilmer's comment was, "Sure, Sonny wants to play as much as I do. It (the competition)will help us because each of us can move the club. We're the same that way. He's the better passer, but we move the club in different ways. There's no animosity between us. We could split the team up if we let it become an unfriendly thing. Winning is the objective, not who's going to play."

But it was a defensive back, Mike Bass, who perhaps came closest to characterizing the two quarterbacks. Bass was talking about the qualities of both men, then he added: "On third and ten I'd rather have Sonny, but on third and two, I'll take Kilmer."

Early in the exhibition season the Skins faced the Denver Broncos. Kilmer played the first half, hit six of 17, including a TD to Jefferson. He put 17 points on the scoreboard. Jurgy then took over and did even better, hitting six of seven for 144 yards and two TD's, including a 65-yard bomb to Tommy Mason. He, too, put 17 points on the board, and after the game George Allen said:

"No team in football has two better quarterbacks than we have."

Both continued to impress right through the season opener in Minnesota when Allen, true to his word, started Billy Kilmer.

In a hard-fought struggle from start to finish, the Redskins were outplayed statistically by the Vikings, but did enough things right to win, 24-21. The next week the team came home to face the Cardinals and when Kilmer came out on the field he received a familiar reception—a chorus of boos. It seems the fans felt in their hearts that a healthy Jurgensen should be the team's quarterback. There were even bumper stickers which called for Sonny's reinstatement.

Against the Cards Kilmer had an average game, yet won, 24-10. Now there was a real clamor for Sonny in

Washington sports circles. Even Billy was forced to comment on the growing issue.

"Let's face it," he said. "There has to be a clear-cut number one for the team's sake. Sometimes a quarterback sees something in the first half that he knows he can exploit in the second half. You can only get the real tempo of the game by going all the way. I'm sure Sonny would say the same thing."

Game number three was played against the lowly New England Patriots in Foxboro, Massachusetts. Billy was good that day. He threw three scoring passes and just missed a fourth when Jefferson was ruled out of bounds after an apparent touchdown catch. But the Patriots didn't quit and they somehow pushed over a late score to upset the Skins by a point, 24-23. Two days later Sonny Jurgensen was practicing with the first unit.

"I knew the day we lost a game I'd be replaced," said Kilmer after Allen announced that Jurgy was returning to the starting spot. "When you don't win, you're replaced; it's as simple as that. I thought I had my best game of the year against the Patriots.

"I'm not bitter with the Washington Fans. Sonny is a great quarterback and they want to see him, just as Jet fans want to see Namath. But I felt I was doing the job." Then he added, "Sonny deserves a chance to play. I've just got to prepare myself as if I were the starter, because you never know what will happen."

Like most great quarterbacks, Jurgensen made the most of his opportunity. He led the Skins to two easy victories, showing that his classic passing form hadn't rusted with inactivity. He was hitting better than ever and it began to look as if Kilmer would never get in again. Then the Skins rolled into Yankee Stadium to play the Giants.

Jurgensen started and ran the offense for 13 plays. On the 14th, he called a little rollout to the right, took the snap and about four steps. Suddenly he pulled up lame, hobbling around in pain. Jurgy had ruptured his achilles tendon. Just like that. He walked slowly to the sideline, finished for the season once more. And without warning, Billy Kilmer was on the field, this time to stay.

Rising to the occasion despite his two-week layoff, Billy threw for two scores and Larry Brown rushed for an incredible 191 yards, as the Skins won the game, 23-16.

The next week, Billy showed everyone that he could do the job again. Facing Joe Namath and the New York Jets, Billy threw a 45-yard TD strike to Jefferson, a 70-yard completion to Taylor, setting up another score, and an 89-yard pass-run TD play to Larry Brown. The Skins won, 35-17, with Kilmer the star once again. After the game, Bill told newsmen how Jurgy's injury enabled him to change his style.

"I was throwing a lot stronger today than if Sonny was there behind me. Then I wouldn't take chances. Without him I can gamble because my position is different psychologically. Without him behind me I can freewheel out there and do things without worrying about the coach jerking me. My guys had confidence they could beat them deep and we did.

"It's just a different thing now knowing the job is mine. If Jurgy's there I might hold back and not zip the ball as hard—or maybe even run instead of throwing. But even if I throw an interception now, I stay in. Period."

In the ensuing weeks, Kilmer led the Skins as well as they'd ever been led. He whipped the Giants, 27-13, connecting on 15 of 23 for 256 yards, and he continued to win after that. In the five games that followed his return, Bill threw for 12 touchdowns, completing 54 of 95 passes for 859 yards,

During the same period the Skins were inside their opponents' 20-yard line 11 times. Billy Kilmer took the team in on all 11 occasions. In four of the five games, Billy brought the Skins from behind for the victory.

"Billy has improved tremendously over the last season," said Ted Marchibroda, the Skins offensive coordinator. "Somehow, last year, I got the impression that Billy didn't think he would stay here. He seems to just have more confidence now."

It was true. Kilmer led the club to six straight wins, seven including the Giant game when Jurgy was hurt. With an 11-1 record, the Skins clinched the Eastern Division title in the NFC. With 1,000-yard runner Larry Brown resting some minor injuries in the final two games, and the team already thinking ahead to the playoffs, the Skins dropped a pair and finished at 11-3.

Billy wound up fourth among NFC passers with 120 completions in 225 attempts for a 53.3 percentage and 1,648 yards. He threw for a big 19 touchdowns and had just 11 intercepted. It might not have been his best year statistically, but it had to be his most satisfying artistically.

Yet the season wasn't complete. There were still the playoffs, and the Skins wanted more than anything else to get into the Super Bowl. That was the goal everyone was pointing to.

Before the first-round playoff game against Green Bay, Billy Kilmer talked about the upcoming weeks.

"We've just got to dedicate ourselves, that's all," he said. "Just three weeks is all it will take, but we'll reap the value of that dedication for the rest of our lives."

Kilmer practiced what he preached against the Packers. He was a master of execution. Calling a tight, ball-control game, Billy had the Skins in command from the outset. With the score tied in the second quarter and the ball on the 32, Billy dropped back and lofted a perfect pass in the direction of Jefferson, who grabbed it on the goal line and went in. That made it 10-3, and the foot of Curt Knight gave the Skins the rest. Washington had a 16-3 victory and went into the NFC finals against Dallas.

Kilmer didn't throw much in the Packer game. He was just seven for 14 for 100 yards. But he did what was necessary. Larry Brown had 101 yards rushing and the two kept the Packer defense hopping.

What Kilmer did to the Cowboys the next week no one expected. Before a huge crowd at RFK Stadium, Kilmer and the Skins came out smoking. Billy had one of the most brilliant days of his career. He started it all with a 15-yard TD strike to Taylor in the second quarter, giving his team a 10-3 halftime lead.

Then in the final period he opened up, hitting Taylor with a neat 45-yard scoring pass to put the icing on the cake. Curt Knight had four field goals and the Redskins were NFC champs, 26-3, as their defense completely shut off the Cowboy attack.

Kilmer was 14 for 18, throwing for 194 yards in a display of passing and leadership that had the whole country talking. In the two weeks preceeding the Skins Super Bowl clash with Miami, everyone learned the Billy Kilmer story. For the first time in his life he was a national celebrity.

The Super Bowl wouldn't be easy. Miami was bidding to become the first team to march through a pro-football season unbeaten in 17 games. They'd already won 16, the first 14 in the regular season and two more in the playoffs. Coach Don Shula had a well-balanced, deep, talented team. They seldom made mistakes, and they never let an opponent's mistake get by them.

The Dolphins feared the Skins and their tandem of Bill Kilmer and Larry Brown. Both had been spectacular in the Packer and Cowboy games.

"Billy Kilmer is what the Washington Redskins are all about," one newspaper story began. Another claimed that in reality Allen preferred Billy at quarterback to Jurgensen because of the way Kilmer stuck to a game plan and just chipped away at the opposition until they crumbled.

That's what he tried to do against the Dolphins. Playing in the Los Angeles Coliseum, where he had seen his first game so many years before, Kilmer tried to repeat his tactics of the other playoff games. He began by trying to establish his running game. It wasn't working. The stout Miami line was wrapping up Larry Brown before he could get started.

So Billy tried some short passes. He only had to throw a couple before he realized something. "I wasn't sharp. I wasn't throwing the ball well." And the Skins weren't moving.

Meanwhile, Miami quarterback Bob Griese was moving his team. In the first period he hit on six straight passes. The fourth pass was a 28-yarder to Howard Twilley that wound up in the end zone for a score. The kick made it 7-0.

The Skins tried to bounce back. Kilmer looked for Larry Brown midway in the second period, but middle linebacker Nick Buoniconti picked the ball off and returned it 32 yards. From there, the Dolphins drove in on the ground, Jim Kiick taking it over, and Miami had a 14-0 halftime lead.

The Skins worked desperately to score. But there was no running game and the Miami zone was laying for Kilmer. One time when Billy had Jerry Smith wide open in the end zone his pass hit the goal post and bounced away.

Not until late in the fourth quarter did the Skins score. And that was on a freak play. The Dolphins were trying a field goal, and a bad pass from center fouled the play. Cornerback Mike Bass picked up the football and raced it into the end zone. That made it 14-7, but there was next to no time left. Miami ran out the clock before the Skins could get the ball back.

It was a tremendous disappointment for everyone. Kilmer himself took the blame, saying he should have passed better. Maybe. But there was no running game to support him. Larry Brown had just 26 yards and that put the pressure on Kilmer. He was 14 for 26 but couldn't connect on the big ones or on the bombs. The Dolphin zone bottled him up.

Allen defended his quarterback. "He got us there," the coach said bluntly, and there was surely a bundle of truth in that statement. Kilmer had been the driving force of the Skins attack ever since Jurgensen limped off the Yankee Stadium turf so many weeks before. Brown, Taylor, Harraway, Jefferson, and many of the other Redskins had outstanding years, but it was the spirit and leadership of Billy Kilmer that could be singled out.

That leadership was still in evidence in 1973, though it was another season of torment for Billy. He ought to be used to it by now. The Skins came back with their two veterans, Kilmer and Jurgensen, but before long Sonny was having knee trouble and Billy stomach problems. The club was also having problems generating the usual running game, putting even more pressure on the quarterbacks.

Billy's problem was an intestinal disorder, a blockage that would need surgery after the season. Yet he played out the season and had an outstanding campaign under the circumstances, completing 122 of 227 passes for 1,656 yards. He threw for 14 TD's and had only nine intercepts.

The Skins weren't quite as potent as the year before, but still finished with a 10-4 mark, tied with Dallas for the divisional title. Dallas had the top spot in the playoffs because of a point advantage and the

Skins, as the wild-card team, had to face the Minnesota Vikings.

In the week before the playoff game Billy Kilmer was in the hospital, being fed through tubes, his stomach problem worsening. He couldn't practice, but he was out there at game time calling the signals.

He led his team coolly and well. The Skins had a 7-3 lead at the half and it was 10-10 after three. Then Fran Tarkenton found his wide receiver John Gilliam on two straight scoring passes to give the Vikes the lead. Playing in pain and with shortness of breath, Kilmer tried to lead the Skins back.

With time running out he drove the club downfield, faded back, and hit Roy Jefferson with a 28-yard TD pass, making the score 27-20. He kept throwing for the tie the final time he had the ball, but the Vikes used a prevent defense and stopped him.

"The real hero of this game was Billy Kilmer," said winning quarterback Frank Tarkenton. "He played when most guys would be in the hospital and he played brilliantly. I can't think of too many other guys who could have done what he did under those conditions."

But playing under adverse conditions is nothing new for Bill. He's been through it all, fighting injuries, fighting for a job, fighting for a Super Bowl. He'll have a new challenge next year from young Joe Theismann, a former Notre Dame star who's been playing in Canada.

Billy Kilmer once said that he never plans ahead. He's seen too many hopes, too many dreams dashed by some unforeseen occurrence. "Out of season I've never been a game-plan type of guy," is the way he put it.

No, he doesn't waste time looking for trouble. But no matter what the future brings, Billy Kilmer has proved time and again that he's ready to face anything.

TERRY BRADSHAW

It was a warm spring day in 1966. The Shreveport Woodlawn High School track team was engaged in a meet with a rival Louisiana school. The main body of the teams as well as most of the spectators were gathered around the oval track, watching the running and jumping events. Off in a far corner of the sprawling field a small group of people gathered for the javelin event.

The young competitors began hurling the spear for distance. Up stepped Shreveport Woodlawn's top thrower, a tall, lanky blond youth with a tough-looking, wiry build. He carefully adjusted his grip on the javelin, then stared straight ahead for a moment before starting his approach.

The big youngster ran with strong, powerful strides. As he neared the take-off line, he went into the final crossover and skip that characterizes perfect javelin form, then released the spear with a loud grunt.

All eyes followed the blue blur and it shot off his arm like a rocket. It seemed to keep rising as if jet propelled. When the other boys' throws began descending, this youngster's was still flying upward and outward. Finally, it began to arc downward. When it hit, its point buried deep in the ground so there could be no mistaking the spot.

Meet officials ran toward the fallen spear. They had not been standing out that far. Now they were excited. A tape measure was brought out. The distance was called off. They got another tape and measured again. Once more the distance was shouted out. Everyone began murmuring excitedly.

"Great toss, Terry."

"Way to chuck that thing, Ter."

"That showed 'em, Terry."

But even in the excitement of the explosive throw, no one quite realized exactly what happened. Terry Bradshaw had just broken the national prep school all-time javelin record with a toss of 244 feet, 11 inches. It beat the old mark by more than 13 feet.

Terry's teammates congratulated him and slapped him on the back. It was the first time that Terry Bradshaw's arm had brought him nationwide recognition, but it wouldn't be the last. Terry could have continued with the javelin and perhaps have become a world-class thrower. But he decided to concentrate on throwing something else, an oblong-shaped sphere made out of pigskin—a football.

Four years later, the same Terry Bradshaw would

capture the national spotlight once again. And this time people other than a handful of track enthusiasts would know who he was. For in that span of time, Terry Bradshaw had honed his football talents to such a fine degree that he became the most talked-about pro football quarterback prospect since Joe Namath.

In Terry's case, it was a remarkable feat. While the likes of Namath, Fran Tarkenton, Billy Kilmer and later Jim Plunkett developed their football skills at great universities like Alabama, Georgia, UCLA, and Stanford, Terry Bradshaw got his gridiron baptism at Louisiana Polytechnic Institute.

What's that, you ask? Well, it's a relatively small university (student body about 8,000) located in Ruston, Louisiana. It plays its football in the Gulf States Conference against such teams as McNeese State, Lamar Tech, the University of Southwest Louisiana, and Northeast Louisiana State. The rest of the slate is similarly unexciting, except to football fans of the region and some footloose pro scouts.

Anyway, that's where Bradshaw played, but it wasn't long before the power attached to his right shoulder began speaking for itself. Anyone with an arm like Terry Bradshaw's would have attracted attention even if he played in no league at all.

A modern version of Jack Armstrong, the All-American boy, Terry was devoutly religious, clean-cut, and clean-living. He seemed to have the world at his feet when he broke a host of passing records at Louisiana Tech. Pro scouts were drooling, pro coaches dreaming . . . when they weren't scheming about ways to get him. With his bright blond hair and handsome face, he was truly a Golden Boy with a golden future.

Bradshaw said he was happy when the Pittsburgh Steelers drafted him, a team that had a 1-13 record the year before he got there. An impressive exhibition season solidified Terry's immediate claim to superstardom. The fans said that his release was quicker then Namath's, that he ran better than Tarkenton, that he was stronger than Gabriel. Perhaps no rookie quarterback in the history of the game has ever had so many words of praise heaped upon him at one time. But then the 1970 season started, and with it the most trying time of Terry Bradshaw's young life.

That life began on September 12, 1948, in Shreveport, Louisiana. Terry was the second of three sons born to Mr. and Mrs. W. M. (Bill) Bradshaw. When Terry was just a toddler, his family made a big move, going to Clinton, Iowa, where Mr. Bradshaw had taken a new job. Terry went through his early grammar school days there.

The Bradshaws remained in Iowa for a few years; then Mr. Bradshaw announced that he was taking the family back to Shreveport, where he became plant manager for the American Machine and Foundry Corporation. Years afterward, Mr. Bradshaw told why he did it:

"One reason I came back was because of sports. I wanted the boys to participate and I knew that Shreveport had a superior junior sports program."

Yet Bill Bradshaw adds a note of caution, lest someone misunderstand his intentions. "I never insisted my boys become athletes," he said frankly. "I hoped they'd be ballplayers, I exposed them to it and I encouraged them. But no one can force a boy into being something he doesn't have a real feeling for."

Terry's older brother, Gary, just a year his senior, was also a fine football prospect until a fall from a tree injured his back permanently. Craig, the youngest, is still only 15 years old. He has a possible future in baseball.

Bill Bradshaw was a sports lover from way back. When he was a kid he hung around with Joe Adcock (later the first baseman with the Milwaukee Braves) and the two were well-known figures on the Louisiana sandlots. When the Pittsburgh Steelers came to Shreveport for an exhibition game in 1952, somehow Bill Bradshaw ended up driving their team bus out to the field. "They gave me $20 for that little ride," he recalls. "The most I ever got from other teams in those days was five dollars, so I've always maintained that the Steelers couldn't be a cheap outfit."

Of course, Bill Bradshaw had no way of knowing that his son would someday be negotiating with that same team, talking turkey at a figure considerably higher than the tip the elder Bradshaw received.

But despite his long association with sports and athletes, Bill Bradshaw was above all a devoted family man. A teetotaller and regular churchgoer, Mr. Bradshaw had always believed in family togetherness. The whole family often participated in after-dinner softball games.

"I always believed in keeping my boys busy," Mr. Bradshaw says, "either with sports or chores. That way, they wouldn't have time to get into trouble. In that respect, I guess I've been a strict father, but I don't feel I've been unreasonable, even though I always rode hard herd on the boys."

Mr. Bradshaw stuck by a set of firm rules. There were school night curfews for the boys, no smoking or drinking, respect for all elders, and no automobiles.

"I always had to know where my boys were," Mr. Bradshaw said, "and you don't know where in the world they are if they're running off in cars."

Though Mr. Bradshaw may seem tough and old-fashioned by today's standards, he stuck to his principles and his boys respected him for it. Right to this day, Terry has no complaints about his home life. In fact, he looks to the love and attention he had as a youth as one of the reasons for his success.

Terry's athletic career began slowly and quietly, but there were enough highlights along the way to indicate that there was something special about this bright youngster. When he was living in Clinton, Iowa, as a nine-year-old, he was picked by the coaches of the Little League to join an all-star team which was set to travel to New York. But Terry's joy quickly turned to disappointment when it was discovered that the boys had to be at least ten to make the trip.

When he was 13, he went to visit his grandmother in Coushatta, Louisiana, for two weeks. During that time he joined a local baseball team and promptly went out and pitched a perfect game. Even then he had the beginnings of that incredible arm.

By the time he entered junior high in Shreveport as a seventh grader, he was ready to play football. But he was small for his age and the coaches wouldn't even issue him a uniform. The next year he was bigger, but there were so many boys with experience that the team again ran out of uniforms before getting around to him.

It was a bitter disappointment for the youngster, but his father advised him not to give up, to believe in himself and keep at it. Then one day he and another youngster who didn't make the team were watching practice. Terry picked up an extra football and began throwing it to the other boy.

"I could throw pretty well, even then," he recalls, "and I told my friend to go out for some long ones. We threw for about 10 minutes or so and I guess the coaches noticed me, because the next day they gave me a uniform."

But that didn't mean they gave him the quarterback job. They made him a linebacker. "I loved it," says Terry now. "I remember one scrimmage when I really felt good. I think I must have made about a dozen unassisted tackles. I figured I had it made. But about a week later I broke my collarbone and missed the whole season."

The injury jinx continued to plague him. The next year, his last at Oak Terrace Junior High, the coaches made him the tailback in a shotgun-type offense, but he separated his shoulder before the first game and didn't return until the final two contests of the season.

"I threw about 50 passes in those two games," he remembers, "and didn't complete a whole lot, but it was a start."

When he arrived at Shreveport Woodlawn High

the next year he was just starting to really grow. "I had a hard time convincing my Woodlawn coaches that I could play varsity ball," he says. "They thought I was too small at first, and even when I started growing I guess they still thought of me as a little guy. I rotated between the varsity and junior varsity in both my sophomore and junior seasons. I think I played in maybe three games with the varsity as a junior. They had a senior quarterback that year, Trey Prather (who later went to LSU and subsequently lost his life in Vietnam), who was breaking all the school passing records, and the coaches let him play as much as they could."

By the time he was a senior Terry could be denied no longer. What's more, the team had just one starter back and had to rebuild. Terry became the quarterback and immediately began firing bullet passes all over the field. With him at the helm, the Woodlawn Knights were winners again, taking the district championship and going all the way to the state finals before losing a tough one to Sulphur High, 12-9.

Terry was a dedicated football player by then, and knew he wanted to concentrate on the sport in college. He came home one day shortly after the season ended and told his father that he was going to forget about track that spring. Bill Bradshaw didn't like to hear that. Terry's arm had been getting stronger all the time and he was beginning to make his mark as a javelin thrower.

"There were two reasons why I wanted him to stick with it," says Mr. Bradshaw. "Naturally, I wanted him busy, but I also felt he had the ability to break the state record in the javelin and I wanted him to fulfill that potential. I asked him to stay on the team, to get that record for me. And that's the only time I ever asked one of my boys to actually do something for me. Terry was a good kid and he agreed."

In the second meet of the season, Terry tossed the spear 222 feet. That throw broke the state record his father had asked him to aim for. And, of course, he didn't stop there. Several weeks later at Bossier City he got off the big one, the toss of 244 feet, 11 inches that broke the national prep school all-time javelin record.

"I was really surprised at the number of cards and letters I got from track fans after breaking the record," he recalls. "There were even some from Europe. People were sending me things to autograph for them, and some guy in Italy even sent me a present. ... I could have had a track scholarship to almost any school in the country, but I knew then that it was time to concentrate on football."

The next problem was picking a college. The track offers were still much more numerous than the football feelers and Terry did not have very many schools to choose from. Finally, he narrowed it down to three schools, Baylor, Louisiana State University, and Louisiana Tech. The first two are big-time outfits where he could surely achieve national recognition. But there was something about Baylor he didn't like (some said it was the sight of whisky bottles in many of the dormitory rooms), and things never worked out with LSU.

In fact, it was because the LSU people hemmed

and hawed for so long that he finally decided on Tech, which was located some 70 miles from his home in Shreveport.

"As far as I'm concerned," Terry said in answering critics who felt he had made a mistake, "Tech plays a real good brand of football. They have a fine coaching staff, use a pro-style offense, and are playing in a new 25,000-seat stadium. If I'm good enough to play pro ball I'll get my chance, no matter which college I attend."

It didn't take Terry long to find admirers. He was just a freshman when a scout saw him for the first time. The man's name was Jim Palmer, and he worked for an organization called BLESTO-V, a talent scouting service which worked collectively for the Bears, Lions, Eagles, Steelers, and Vikings.

Anyway, Palmer watched the youngster throw a football for the first time and quickly filled out a report which read in part, "He has the best arm I've ever seen on a freshman quarterback."

Palmer returned in May, when Terry was in the midst of spring practice with the varsity. He was still a freshman, but the scout was already looking to next year. "This youngster has the quickest delivery and strongest arm I've ever seen on a sophomore." Then he added a negative note. "He doesn't scramble well and needs experience." What did anyone expect? Terry was still green behind the ears, though he had seen some varsity action as a frosh.

The club was young and inexperienced itself. Terry was the number two quarterback but didn't really see much action as a frosh in 1966. He was in long enough to throw 81 passes, completing 34 for a 42.0 percentage and 404 yards. He failed to throw a TD pass, however, and had three picked off. The club's 1-9 record and 83 points scored indicated its entire caliber of play.

After the season, Joe Aillet, Tech's coach of 26 years, retired, and Maxie Lambright took his place. Also coming with Lambright as an assistant was Mickey Slaughter, a former Tech signalcaller who played four years with the Denver Broncos of the American Football League. Terry always gives Slaughter much of the credit for his development.

"I built up my arm by lifting weights," he said, "a lot of weights. And plenty of throwing helped me, too. But, basically, it was Coach Slaughter who made me mentally tough. I may have had the physical ability when I first came to Tech, but I didn't have the confidence needed to make an offense go. Someone had to give me the drive and that's what Coach Slaughter did. He drove the confidence into me."

The confidence didn't come overnight. Terry was an alternate quarterback his sophomore year of 1967, as the team began rebuilding under Coach Lambright. The Bulldogs had a couple of big wins, 34-7 over Delta State, and 41-31 against Lamar Tech. But there were losses, too, including a season-ending 58-7 rout at the hands of Southern Mississippi. When it ended, the Bulldogs were 3-7. All they could do was hope their young players would come of age in '68.

As for Terry, he began to show the passing form that was to make him a national celebrity in less than two years. He threw the football 139 times, completing 78 for 981 yards and a 56.1 percentage. He fired his first three touchdown passes, but on the other side had 10 picked off. He still had to learn when to run and when to eat the ball.

When Terry returned for his junior year of 1968 he finally knew the quarterback job was his. He'd be calling the plays and running the Bulldog offense. And it wasn't long before he opened up. He was 13 for 30 and 216 yards in an opening victory over Mississippi State, 20-13. The next week he was a conservative, hitting on just eight of 15 for 105 yards and a score, as Tech whipped East Carolina, 35-7.

Then in the following two weeks, Terry really began putting on an aerial show. He was 20 of 38 for 319 yards and three scores against McNeese State, and then made the fans' eyes pop with a scintillating 28 of 47 for 432 yards and two scores against Southwestern Louisiana. Unfortunately, the Bulldog defense wasn't equal to the task, and Tech lost both games, 27-20 and 28-24. So when the club faced Northwestern State the following week, they were determined not to lose another.

"We figured the success of our season hinged on that game," said Terry. "Some people were calling us chokers, and rapping the defense. But let's face it, it's a team effort and everyone's to blame for a loss."

It was the 53rd meeting between the two teams, so if anyone is wondering how long these small Louisiana schools have been playing the grid game, there's the answer. Anyway, it was a wild contest all the way. Northwestern dominated the first half as Terry could complete just two of 12 passes in a performance that had people shaking their heads.

Tech had a 7-0 lead mostly on running plays, with Terry completing one 13-yard pass which brought the ball to the two. Minutes after the score, the Golden Boy was nailed in his own end zone for a safety, and a subsequent Northwestern score made it 9-7. It was a 19-7 game at the half and the Bulldogs looked like they were going down to a third straight defeat.

But in the third period, Terry began hitting. He found Tommy Spinks open for passes of 10 and 13 yards, then rocketed one to Larry Brewer in the end zone for a score. Northwestern upped its lead to 26-14 before Tech drove downfield again, with long runs by its halfbacks. Terry then took it over from the one and the kick made it 26-21. Another Tech score minutes later made it a 28-26 game, with the Bulldogs out in front once again.

Terry got a third TD on a sneak, but the Tech defense again weakened. The Demons scored twice to go ahead by 39-35 with less than three minutes left. Tech got the ball and Terry tried to start another drive. But when he tried a pass over the middle it was picked off by a State defender. With just 2:42 left in the game, it seemed that State had won.

Only this time the Bulldog defense held, and Northwestern was forced to punt. The kick by Larry Smith was returned a few yards to the Tech 18 by Butch Danile. Bradshaw re-entered the game with his team 82 yards from paydirt and just 25 seconds remaining. There was time for one play, perhaps two.

Terry took the snap and dropped straight back.

Northwestern had its linemen charging and Bradshaw knew he didn't have much time. He waited until the last possible second, then fired hard and long over the middle. Flanker Ken Liberto ran under the ball at the Demon 40 and suddenly was in the clear, racing all the way to the end zone to complete the dramatic, 82-yard play. Louisiana Tech had won, 42-39.

As for Terry, he had returned from a disastrous first half to complete 11 of 15 second-half passes in leading his team to a great win. And the game turned the season around just as Terry had said it would. Tech went on to take its final five games. The Bulldogs finished with an 8-2 mark and the Gulf States Conference title.

Terry Bradshaw had rewritten the Bulldog record book. During 1968 he completed 176 of 339 passes for a whopping 2,890 yards. His completion percentage was 51.9 and he rifled 22 touchdown passes to his waiting receivers. Just 15 of his throws were intercepted.

Interestingly enough, five of those interceptions came in one game, against Northwestern Louisiana, and they served to show just what kind of a competitor Terry Bradshaw was.

On four of the five occasions it was Bradshaw who busted through blockers to make the tackle. And he hit the ballcarriers so hard that he broke the collarbone of one of them.

"I like the physical side of football," he admitted one day. "I like being hit. I've seen a lot of quarterbacks, even in pro ball, who seem quiet, almost passive on the field. When they get hit they just lie there. They don't even get mad. But when I get hit, I get very mad."

There were times at Tech when Coach Lambright had to send in messengers, not with plays, but with orders for Terry to cool it, to stop seeking out contact and to run out of bounds when he saw he'd be hit. The temptation to lower his head and plow into a defender was always great.

The season wasn't yet over for Terry and the Bulldogs. Their fine record earned them a bid to the Grantland Rice Bowl against Akron University. While the game didn't compare in glamor or importance to the Rose or Orange Bowls, both teams were nevertheless ready to give it everything they had.

It was a cold December 14 when the two clubs met at Murfreesboro, Tennessee, but it didn't take long for Terry Bradshaw to warm up the air with his passing.

The Bulldogs began driving as soon as they got the ball. Bradshaw took them downfield by mixing his throwing with running plays and keepers. With the ball on the 16 he dropped back, then took off and scrambled by several Akron players for the score.

Minutes later he struck again, hitting Tommy Spinks with a 36-yard scoring pass, and before the quarter ended, Buster Herren banged over from the two, giving Tech a 21-0 lead.

Akron came back with touchdowns in the second period Terry began hitting again, culminating one drive with a six-yard pass to Larry Brewer, and a sec- and third quarters, making it 21-13, but in the final ond by scrambling over himself from the eight. Witnesses claim that he completed one pass after being hit by six different Akron players, with three still hanging onto him when he threw.

The final score was 33-13, and Terry Bradshaw won the Most Valuable Player Award hands down. He had completed 19 of 33 passes for 261 yards and two scores. In addition, he gained 71 yards on 12 running plays, though that statistic was modified by 36 yards lost trying to pass. But when he ran, he did it well.

After the bowl game Terry could sit back and watch the honors roll in. And there were many. He was the Player of the Year in the Gulf States Conference; the Most Valuable Player at Louisiana Tech; a first team all-America selection by the American Football Coaches Association; the Athlete of the Year in the Gulf States Conference as voted by the Louisiana Sports Writers Association.

That wasn't all. By the end of his junior year, Terry Bradshaw had become one of the most heavily scouted quarterback prospects in the country. At 6-3, 215 pounds, he had the size and strength to play in the pros, and no one ever questioned the quality of his arm.

When Terry returned for his senior year, it was like an anticlimax. What more could he do for an encore? He was already NCAA college division total offense leader (2,987 yards in 426 plays).

Terry had a multitude of laudatory nicknames, perhaps the most popular being "The Rifleman," given him for two reasons—his arm and his facial resemblance to actor Chuck Connors, who played in a TV series of that name. Indeed, his square-jawed, high-cheekboned appearance, complete with a cleft in his chin, made him a very handsome football player.

And once the season opened, his opponents knew that success hadn't gone to Terry Bradshaw's head. He took up right where he left off—pitching strikes. Three TD's against East Carolina highlighted the opening win (final score: 24-6) and that was just the beginning.

In the third game against Southwestern Louisiana, Terry hit 15 of 25 for 207 yards and ran for another 68 on 10 tries to highlight an easy victory. Then in the fifth game against Chattanooga, Terry played barely one half, hitting nine of 10 for 209 big yards and three TD's. In fact, the stadium transformers failed and the game had to be halted for some 88 minutes. Some joked that it was Bradshaw's lightning that shortcircuited the lights. One pro scout on hand, John Carson of the Eagles, was really impressed by Terry's cool that night.

"I watched him throw a 20-yard touchdown pass and then all the lights went out," Carson said. "The place was dark for almost an hour and a half. When the lights came on again, Bradshaw came back onto the field and threw a 76-yard touchdown pass on the very first play. I couldn't believe how cool he was about it."

The whole season was cool. Tech lost just once, a 24-23 squeaker at the hands of Southern Mississippi. Included in their fine 8-1 record was a smashing 77-40 triumph over Lamar Tech, which broke several school and conference marks. Terry was 17 of 33 in that one, for a big 316 yards. The team returned to the Grantland Rice Bowl again in 1969, this time facing East Tennessee. That one was a mild upset. East Tennessee defenders overwhelmed the Bulldog lines and rapped Terry 12 times for 143 yards in losses. He still managed to complete 20 of 39 for 299 yards, but Tech lost, 34-14.

Thus ended the college career of Terry Bradshaw. He wasn't quite as busy his senior year. Many games were won early and he managed some bench time. He nevertheless completed 136 of 248 for 2,314 yards and 14 scores. That gave him a career total of 463 completions in 879 attempts for a mammoth total of 7,149 yards. His passing percentage for four years was 52.7, and he fired away for 42 touchdowns.

This time his all-America honors weren't restricted to the small college division—although he copped all the top prizes in that division. He was a first-team selection of the American Coaches Association and *Time* Magazine, and made the second team in the *Sporting News* poll. And, of course, he was once again Gulf States Conference Athlete of the Year.

While Terry Bradshaw was rewriting the record books at Louisiana Tech, the wheels were turning elsewhere. The wheels that drive the huge complex known as the National Football League. The men who know football best had been watching Terry for some time already, and their comments were as splendid as Terry's best bullet pass.

Gil Brandt, chief scout of the Dallas Cowboys, didn't mince any words in talking about tall Terry. "He's tremendous," said Brandt. "He's got to be a first-round choice for sure. I think he'll be the first quarterback picked. In fact, it wouldn't surprise me if he was the first player drafted. Just look at what he has. He can really throw the football. He's got a real quick, accurate delivery. And he's strong with good speed."

The Cowboys' receiver coach, Ray Renfro, echoed the sentiment. "He's got to be the best I've seen this year. His arm is so strong that he doesn't have to have perfect balance when he's throwing. He could really fit into our system. It makes me sick to know we don't have a chance to get him." Renfro was aware that Bradshaw would be drafted long before the Cowboys' first chance to pick came around.

Then Brandt elaborated more, comparing Terry with some of the other top QB's who would be available in the upcoming draft.

"There are some real good quarterbacks available this year," the scout said. "Some people think Mike Phipps of Purdue is the best. Archie Manning of Mississippi is a good one, so is Bill Cappleman of Florida State. But to tell the truth, I'd take Bradshaw over any one of them. I just think he's a better football player.

"Of course, a guy like Phipps has that Big Ten experience. He's been in the Rose Bowl and has proven himself a winner. There's a big difference between that and playing in the Gulf States Conference. But Bradshaw has the greater potential.

"What it amounts to is that someone will have to make a decision like we did when we drafted Calvin Hill out of Yale. They can take Bradshaw over Phipps and learn three years later if they were right."

The Colts' George Young watched Bradshaw in action several times and gave the youngster (and the team drafting him) his blessing.

"There's really no risk in drafting Bradshaw," he said. "He's tall enough, strong enough, and fast enough. He's got the arm and the intelligence. Add to that good poise, ability to avoid rushers, and a propensity to move a ballclub. What else do you want in a quarterback?"

Former Colt defensive back Carl Taseff, also scouting at the time, watched Terry fire one pass and said, "I've seen enough. Just look at the speed on the ball. And look at his hands. They're like ham hocks."

That was just a sampling. Former Giants' coach Jim Lee Howell called Terry a "big Sammy Baugh," and one-time quarterback great Y. A. Tittle said "they ought to charge admission just to watch him warm up."

The stage seemed set for a first-round draft. But just to show that he could play with the big boys, Terry accepted invitations to participate in The North-South Game and then in the Senior Bowl game, both post-season affairs that always attract the top college players and pro prospects in the country.

Terry journeyed to Miami for the North-South game that was set for Christmas Day. Mike Phipps was slated to start for the North team, and Terry would be battling Florida State's Bill Cappleman for the starting job on the South Side. The South's coach was Bill Peterson of Florida State, and that gave Terry an early line on just who the starter would be.

The scouts watched the practice sessions intently.

When it began to look as if Cappleman would start for the South, Ace Parker of Duke, one of the BLESTO-V scouts, commented, "Look at Bradshaw's delivery! He's really impressive. Cappleman isn't nearly as quick as he is."

Another interested spectator at Miami was Chuck Noll, the youthful coach of the Pittsburgh Steelers. Pittsburgh had just completed a dreadful 1-13 season, the same as the Chicago Bears, and the two teams flipped a coin to see which would get the number one draft choice. The Steelers won. That meant Chuck Noll had a lot of quick decisions to make.

First of all, he wasn't sure if he wanted to draft a quarterback. He had played a rookie in 1969, Terry Hanratty of Notre Dame, a Pennsylvania-born lad who seemed like the right man to run the team in the 1970's. But Hanratty hadn't really impressed, so Noll still kept an open mind. He also had good reports on Phipps, San Diego State's Dennis Shaw, and Bradshaw.

"I had never seen Terry in person before I went to Miami," Noll recalls, "but the minute I saw him walk onto the practice field I thought to myself, 'He's an athlete.' Then I watched him begin throwing. I was really startled. I knew from the films that he had a strong arm, but film doesn't measure intensity. He really winged it in there."

Unfortunately, Terry suffered a hamstring pull that day and it slowed him down a bit. It also gave Peterson the final reason to start his own boy, Cappleman. Terry played part of the second and fourth quarters, and ran the team well. When someone asked him if the hamstring bothered him, Terry exploded, "Bull!" he said. "I didn't play more because the coach wanted Cappleman in there. Now I'm going to Mobile for the Senior Bowl and I'm going to beat him (Cappleman) out."

Back in Pittsburgh, Chuck Noll and his staff watched the game on television, then studied the films. "We weren't convinced. Phipps hadn't done much, either, while Dennis Shaw had been the MVP of another all-star game, so it was still a three-way race."

In between the North-South and the Senior Bowl, Terry jumped into a lesser game that was covered by Steeler defensive line coach Walt Hackett. Hackett came back to Pittsburgh and brashly announced to Noll, "Bradshaw's the guy!"

By now, Noll was thinking more and more about drafting one of the quarterbacks, and he hopped a plane to Mobile five days before the Senior Bowl game.

The coaches timed the players in the 40-yard dash. Terry sprinted the distance in 4.7 seconds, very good time for quarterback. But in doing that, he pulled the hamstring muscle again and his coach, Don Shula, offered to let him sit the game out. Terry wouldn't hear of it.

"I went down to Mobile to beat out Cappleman, win the position, start, and have a good game. Nothing was going to stop me."

That's what really impressed Noll. He watched Terry in practice, setting up and throwing despite the injury, responding to top-flight competition like a pro.

In the game itself, Terry started and played very

well, winging his passes with authority and hitting his receivers. In the third quarter he was hit hard and suffered two broken ribs. Yet he continued to play. The game ended in a 27-27 tie. Terry had completed 17 of 31 passes for 267 yards and two TD's, and was named the game's Most Valuable Player. Now the Steelers had settled on Bradshaw as the man. Their only remaining question was whether to trade him for established players, or make him their quarterback.

There were several things to take into consideration. First of all, many pro teams began making offers to the Steelers even before the draft. "We've had some fantastic offers," was the way vice-president Dan Rooney of the Steelers put it. "We've got to assess them."

And Pete Retzlaff, the general manager of the Eagles and one of the men who admitted to making an offer, said, "O. J. Simpson might have gotten more publicity last year, but internally within the league, there's much more talk about Bradshaw. He's evidently a quarterback who can run your team, and run it right now."

That was a major factor. The other was the Steeler organization. It had a very bad history of getting rid of quarterbacks who later became superstars. Just listen to the list of throwers who began in the Pittsburgh organization and were shipped out before they could develop. It begins with Sid Luckman and from there moves to John Unitas, Earl Morrall, Jack Kemp, Len Dawson, and Bill Nelson. That's amazing. All of them became outstanding signalcallers. The Steelers didn't want that to happen again with Bradshaw.

On the other hand, the Steelers had to consider the quarterbacks who had previously been the number one choice of the entire league. The list reads like a who's-who of forgotten men—Boley Dancewicz, Harry Gilmer, King Hill, Randy Duncan, George Shaw, Terry Baker, Bobby Garrett, and Bill Wade. None of them made it. True, Paul Hornung was another first-choice quarterback, but he found his greatest success at halfback.

The Steelers tried to ignore all those factors. They just looked at Terry as a football player. With offers coming in right up to draft time, the Steelers made their decison. They picked Terry Bradshaw.

"I'm thrilled to death," was Terry's first reaction. "I had a hunch I might go high, maybe first round. But being the number one pick is the most exciting thing that's ever happened to me."

Now Terry had to negotiate his contract with the Steelers. Taking some advice from Roman Gabriel and his dad, Terry decided to do his own negotiating with help from a personal friend, a local attorney from Shreveport. He stayed away from the high-powered agents who had come into vogue about that time.

Slowly, he began to see himself within a much larger scheme of things.

"I was very happy to be chosen by the Steelers," he said. "I wanted to go to a losing team all along. That way, if the team became a winner they'd do it with me. From the first time I went to Pittsburgh and met some of the guys and the coaches, I knew the Steelers were a team in search of a leader. That's what I'm going to be paid for . . . to be a leader."

On one of his early trips to Pittsburgh, Terry went out for a night on the town with veteran linebacker Andy Russell. Terry asked Russell just how he thought the veterans would accept him.

"You'll probably get your share of needling," Russell answered.

The blond bomber bristled slightly. "Look," he told the vet. "I'm a leader. If anyone gives me trouble in the huddle—and I don't care who they are—I'm going to sting them."

Russell was impressed, just as everyone else was by the youngster's confidence. Before long he had signed his contract, a six-figure package, estimated in the $200,000 to $300,000 range. He was well satisfied. He was also beginning to reap the reward of being an instant "personality."

In February he went to New York to model for a picture layout in *Harper's Bazaar* magazine. The story was designed to show how women's fashions were influenced by sports. Other male models were rather well known, men like Arthur Ashe, Mark Spitz, and Bob Hope. But when it came to football, editor Gloria Moncouer wanted a new face.

"Joe Namath was too old, too overphotographed," she said. "As soon as I saw all the pictures of Terry Bradshaw in the papers I knew I wanted him. I wanted those blue eyes to show."

Terry described the whole experience as "exciting." Yet he is a man who never loses his sense of reality.

Not even the instant celebrity treatment could change his basic nature.

Still a devout Baptist and already a longtime member of the Fellowship of Christian Athletes, Terry continued doing volunteer church work in the summer, acting as a youth director for underprivileged kids.

"I've always said that I'm a Christian who happened also to be an athlete," he once told a reporter. "Any time I have the chance to speak to kids I tell them that everyone isn't selected to be the same thing in life. Whether it's an athlete, or something else, you've got to accept it for what it is.

"I always figured it this way. It was the Lord who gave me this body and strong arm and if the arm went dead on me tomorrow, it would just be Him taking it back. I believe—and believe strongly—in God, and I don't think it's a cornpone thing."

So Terry was his own man and seemed to know where he was going. When he got to the Steeler camp, it soon became obvious that his main competition would be Terry Hanratty. The other quarterbacks, Dick Shiner and Kent Nix, would soon be on their way to other teams. Hanratty was less than impressive his rookie year of '69. He had trouble handling the big pass rush and hitting his receivers. He connected on just 52 of 126 attempts, a 41.3 average, for 716 yards and eight touchdowns. Thirteen of his passes were picked off. So the battle for the top job would be a wide-open affair between the two Terrys.

By the time the exhibition season rolled around, Coach Noll was alternating his two quarterbacks.

Hanratty played the first and third quarter in the opener against the Dolphins, with Bradshaw relieving in the second and fourth. Miami won the game, 16-10, but it was Bradshaw, as usual, who did most of the impressing.

Blond Terry completed nine of 19 passes, with another five dropped by receivers not used to the velocity with which he threw. He engineered Pittsburgh's only touchdown drive.

"I wasn't really pleased with my performance," he said later. "I made a lot of dumb rookie mistakes and didn't do a good job of reading defenses."

Then Terry admitted that something happened in the huddle that he kind of expected. "On the second play of the second series I ran, they all came back yakking and laughing it up. I felt they were testing me, but it made me mad. As a rule I don't like to cuss anyone out, but this time I said, 'Let's cut out the damn fooling around and get down to business.' They were quiet for the rest of the time I played."

Miami coach Don Shula didn't agree with Terry's critical self-analysis. After the game the Dolphin mentor said, "I've been a Bradshaw man all along. He's tough and strong and has a great arm. Plus he's a remarkable athlete."

Chuck Noll agreed. He wanted to take a longer look at his rookie and played him all the way the next week against Minnesota. All Terry did was complete 12 passes and lead his club to a 20-13 victory. He was progressing right on schedule.

The following week the Steelers came into Pittsburgh for their first game in brand-new Three Rivers

Stadium. They were facing old rivals, the New York Giants, and Terry once again had the nod as the starting quarterback.

This time he was really hot. Directing the Steeler offense like a 10-year veteran, he quickly got his club on the board with two early touchdowns. The second was a beauty, a 37-yard touchdown strike to rookie Ron Shanklin and the crowd went wild.

When Bradshaw came to the sideline to give way to Hanratty they screamed for his return, and they got him again in the second half, as he continued to lead his club to an easy, 21-6, win. Along the way he completed 15 of 23 passes for 244 yards, and he used his ground game very well to keep the young Giant defense off-balance. He was beginning to compile some impressive pro statistics.

"How far can a team go with a rookie quarterback?" Chuck Noll asked himself after the game. Then he answered his own question. "I really don't know. But this is a different kind of rookie."

Giants' quarterback Frank Tarkenton, who sat out the game with a pulled muscle, had plenty of time to evalutate Bradshaw's performance. "He's got a lot of ability and he's sure a good thrower," said Fran the Scram. "Still, it's too early to make a real judgement because he has so much to learn."

As for Terry, it was like a dream come true. "The new stadium ... we won ... my girl was there. It was all beautiful. I wasn't nervous at all today. I started seeing more things out there, especially my secondary receivers. I was looking and I was reading, and that's what it's all about."

Terry's girl was Melissa Babish, Miss Teenage America in 1969. They began dating in 1970 and were married in April of 1972.

As the season neared, Terry was brimming with confidence. "They way I feel," he told the press, "there isn't anyone in the world who can move this club like I can. Really, I can just feel it."

The pre-season statistics bore out his prediction. He had truly moved them more effectively than Hanratty. The team had won four straight exhibitions after the loss to Miami, including a convincing win over the rugged Oakland Raiders, and Terry was instrumental in every one of them. He completed 51 percent of his pre-season passes for 663 yards and three scores. His arm and running ability continued to impress people, and his confidence made everyone believe that the Steelers could win. It was a team that had not taken any kind of title in some 38 years and the fans were hungry. They could wait until the opener against Houston rolled around.

Besides Bradshaw, rookie Shanklin and Dave Smith gave the club two fine receivers, while John Fuqua and Preston Pearson were more than adaquate runners. Both lines were improving, but many of the young players lacked important experience. Still, many predicted a .500 year or better, which was quite optimistic in view of the 1-13 finish of the year before.

Bradshaw's goals were simple. "I want to be the greatest passer who ever played," he said. "I want to be the best quarterback in the game."

But there were some tough nuts to crack in the

Oiler game. Terry would be throwing to three rookie receivers, and they'd be going against a very rough secondary. Terry wanted to strike fast. On the second play of the game he lofted a long pass toward Hubie Bryant. If he connected it would have been a touchdown. But he missed.

After that, everything seemed wrong. Either his passes were dropped by nervous receivers or they wobbled and missed their mark. Perhaps he was nervous, too. Shanklin got free in the second quarter, but the ball slipped off Terry's hand. Instead of a bullet, it was a floater, and the receiver had to stop and wait for it. Another sure touchdown went down the drain.

On the other hand, Houston was doing a nice job. Speedy Jerry Levias caught two TD passes and the Oilers had a 16-0 lead midway in the third period. Bradshaw's passes were still way off the mark, and Noll finally made a decision. He sent Terry Hanratty into the game. The hometown Pittsburgh fans were shocked to silence.

When it ended, Houston had won, 19-7, with Hanratty leading the Steelers to their only score. Bradshaw had had a miserable afternoon, completing just four of 16 for 70 yards. His brilliant exhibition season seemed like a memory from the distant past. Even he couldn't understand what happened.

"I felt so good out there," he said. "Then I did so poorly. I can't figure it out. All those people expected so much. I thought I was loose and relaxed, but nothing seemed to work."

The next week the team traveled to Denver. Terry

was back at the helm for a second chance. Surely, it had just been a bad game, nothing more.

Statistically, the Denver game was better, but not the outcome. The Broncos won, 16-13, as Terry completed 13 of 26 passes for 211 yards. But none of his tosses went for scores. He came out of the game only when he was momentarily racked up by tackle Dave Costa—he was "getting his bell rung," as the pros say. But there were still a lot of mistakes.

Against Cleveland the next week Terry had a similar day. He hit on 13 of 29 for 207 yards, but he had three picked off and didn't throw a score. The Browns won, 15-7. Bradshaw was simply not taking his team into the end zone. He couldn't take it in from the five, the 10, or the 12, and that's losing football.

"I'm having trouble with my passing form," he said. "I'm just not setting up right and there's no zip on the ball. I haven't been throwing the way I did in college."

The next game was against Buffalo, and Pittsburgh finally won one, 23-10. Yet Terry was only three for 12 for 24 yards. Hanratty played a good part of the game and was instrumental in the victory. It began to look as if Noll would alternate his quarterbacks the rest of the way.

After four games, the man with the golden arm had completed just 33 passes in 83 attempts for a 39.8 percentage. He hadn't thrown for a single score and had been intercepted five times. In addition, he was dropped for a safety in each of the first three games. His performance on the heels of the fine exhibition season was a complete mystery.

The next week Terry tossed his first TD, a 67-yard bomb to Ron Shanklin and it gave Pittsburgh a 7-3 win over Houston. Then the word came out of the Steeler camp that the quarterback had been fined for missing a squad meeting. He had returned to Louisiana to visit his ailing mother and failed to make it back on time.

Then, two weeks later, the bottom fell out of Terry Bradshaw's season. He had been 12 for 27 for only 138 yards and four intercepts in a 31-14 loss to Oakland. Then, playing against Cincinnati, he couldn't do anything right, hitting just four of 12 for 40 yards. Noll yanked him early and Hanratty came on to lead the club to a 21-10 victory.

After the game, Terry lost his cool for the first time. Talking to reporters well within earshot of Hanratty, Terry said, "I don't want to play second fiddle to Terry Hanratty. I wouldn't mind if it was someone older, someone ready to retire, but I sure won't play behind someone my age. If the Steelers are planning on that, they better trade me."

The pop-off was ill-timed and even more ill-conceived. Noll was visibly upset and simply retorted by saying that "Terry has a lot of growing up to do, both on and off the field."

A Steeler player, who preferred to remain anonymous, told a Pittsburgh sports writer a few days later what the rest of the players thought of Bradshaw. "I think Terry lost the respect of some guys when he made the crack about being traded and rapped Hanratty. Heck, Hanratty never once griped when Noll played Bradshaw. He took it like a pro, and as a veteran, he probably had more reason to gripe than Bradshaw did."

Nothing worked well after that. Terry didn't even get into the game against the New York Jets the following week. Hanratty went all the way and the club won, 21-17. From that point on, with the exception of one other game, Hanratty was the starter with Bradshaw pitching relief. According to one story, Bradshaw's frustration grew so great that he went out to his car after one game and cried.

Seasoned observers could sense the team's on-field attitude changing. "The blocking appeared crisper, the holes a little wider when Hanratty ran the team," one said.

There were some incredibly bad days, like a three-for-20 afternoon against Green Bay and a three-for-12 outing against Atlanta. In the finale against Philadelphia, Terry didn't play long enough to throw a single pass.

Terry was a hero just once, in the second game with Cleveland. He completed just four of nine, but they were long ones, going for 197 yards and two TD's. The team won that one, 28-9. Otherwise, all the games were losses, and when it was over the Steeler record was 5-9, and that was after a 4-4 start.

The final statistics were appalling. Terry Bradshaw, the most talked about rookie since Namath, had completed just 83 of 218 passes for 1,410 yards. His passing percentage was an atrocious 38.1. He threw just six TD's, was intercepted 24 times and sacked 25 times. Hanratty didn't do much better with percentages. Yet his experience showed as he threw just eight intercepts and was sacked only three times. He had five TD passes.

If someone wanted to make a direct comparison with rookie Namath, Broadway Joe's 1965 stats read 164 completions in 340 attempts, a percentage of 47.2, with 2,220 yards gained, 18 touchdowns, and just 15 intercepts. It was quite a difference.

Asked about his season, Terry had to be honest. "I wouldn't want another year like it for anything in the world. But on the other hand, I got much of the experience I needed. I created a bad press with my mouth and bad performance with my arm.

"As the season went on I was losing confidence steadily. I just wasn't doing my job. When it was over, I just wanted to get away from Pittsburgh as fast as I could. I wanted to go home, stay away from football so I could relax and get the season out of my mind."

Fortunately, the young mind is capable of bouncing back. By February, Terry reported that he was mentally ready and anxious for the new season to start. "This time I'd have to beat out Hanratty on my own. If I didn't produce on the field, he'd play and well deserve it. I just had to be in the right frame of mind, despite the terrible letdown of my rookie year.

"To be honest, I thought I could do it all in one year, I really did. I didn't realize that in pro football you start from scratch. You have to relearn everything from the very beginning. It's a brand new ballgame all the way."

Terry did a lot of thinking during the off-season. Pretty soon, he began seeing stories in the newspapers, stories which were building up another quarterback, Jim Plunkett of Stanford, who would be entering his rookie year with the New England Patriots. The adjectives were all so similar to those used to describe Terry the year before. The stories had a familiar ring.

In May, a reporter asked Terry if he had any advice for young Plunkett, or for that matter, for any upcoming rookie quarterback.

"It'll be one of those years," said, "in that they'll be great days and bad days. But the secret is to keep cool, not let the bad days eat at you for too long. That's the thing I didn't do last year.

"I wouldn't trade my rookie year for anything. But I really wouldn't want to ever go through that again. Of course, I would have been better off if I kept my mouth shut. That's part of keeping your cool. Then if you keep studying and keep learning, you'll be all right.

"There's just so much football to learn. That's the important thing. If you throw an interception, forget it. If you have a bad game and they boo you, forget it."

As for the rest of his season, Terry had other regrets, like popping off about playing behind Hanratty and causing a split in the team. Yet he maintained that it was his basic determination that caused the ill-timed remarks.

"I'm not ashamed of the content of those remarks," Terry confessed. "I wouldn't want to play behind Bart Starr or Roman Gabriel, either. It just so happens that Hanratty's the guy here. My tone and timing may have been all wrong, but I meant what I said in that I don't intend to sit the bench. I plan on being the quarterback of the Steelers, the starting quarterback, and that's the only way I can look at it."

Once training camp opened at St. Vincent College in Latrobe, Pennsylvania, it was obvious that Terry was out to prove himself once more. His tremendous physical assets once again made him the man Pittsburgh seemed to be depending on. Forgetting the disciplinary incidents of the first year, Coach Noll went back to praising his handsome young signalcaller.

"He can stick the ball in there like nobody else," said Noll.

And John Fuqua, the Steelers top runner, indicated that the rest of the squad had forgotten the uneasiness of the previous season. All they were thinking about was football.

"A lot of things confused Terry last year," said Fuqua. "But now when you stand with him in the huddle at practice you can see there's a difference. He calls the defenses and is seeing more things, like where the linebackers are moving. He didn't notice these things at all last year."

Noll also pointed out an interesting statistic about the club. "Our passing percentage as a team was just 38 percent last year, but our average gain per completion was the best in the league. So our quarterbacks were doing something right. We know we can strike for distance. Now we need greater consistency, especially in short-yardage situations."

In an exhibition game against arch-rival Cincinnati, Terry moved the club well, but still had trouble with the inconsistency. He got the only Steeler touchdown on a short run, but also got his bell rung in the fourth quarter, prompting a couple of Bengal defenders to say that he was running the ball too much. "If he keeps doing that, he'll really get hurt," said tackle Steve Chomyszak.

The Steelers finished the exhibition season with a 3-2 mark, but when the club opened the regular season against Chicago, it looked suspiciously like 1970 all over again. Bradshaw was named the starter after another fine preseason, but somehow he caught a case of the jitters again when it began for real.

He completed just 10 of 24 passes for 129 yards. He failed to throw for a touchdown and had four of his tosses picked off by an alert Chicago secondary. Still, it took two fumble recoveries in the last four minutes for the Bears to push across the scores that gave them a 17-15 victory.

After the game, Noll reaffirmed Bradshaw as his number one quarterback, claiming that Hanratty was strictly a backup performer. He also said that the news media buildup was hurting Terry's game. The only encouraging part of the Bear game was that the Steelers won the battle of statistics.

The next week against Cincinnati they won, 21-10, with Terry connecting on 18 of 30 passes for 249 yards. He hit Dave Smith with a 16-yard TD toss, then flipped a 13-yarder to Preston Pearson. When Terry came back with a 15-of-24 performance in a win over San Diego, it was beginning to look as if he was finally finding the touch.

He completed 12 of 27 against Cleveland, 20 of 39 versus Kansas City, 21 of 32 against Houston, and 20 of 35 when the Steelers met Baltimore. Bradshaw was much better, yet the club's record was 3-4. There were still a few holes to be filled, especially on defense, and it didn't appear as if the team would do much better than that. Yet some experts saw the potential and began counting the Steelers as one of the clubs with a bright future.

There were some inconsistencies in the second half of the year. In a big win over Cleveland, Terry completed just four of 11 for 70 yards, before being replaced by Hanratty. He came back to have a tremendous 25-of-36 day against the Dolphins, throwing for three scores before Miami pulled it out in the final seconds. But he was just six of 17 against Denver and 14 of 31 versus Houston. That prompted his only benching of the season. But he came off the bench to throw fourth-quarter touchdowns to Fuqua and Ron Shanklin in a 21-13 upset of the Bengals.

Coming into their final game, the Steelers were 6-7. They wanted a win, so that they would have a .500 season. But they'd be playing the powerful Los Angeles Rams, and it wouldn't be easy.

In the Cincinnati game, Hanratty fractured a collarbone. Noll had used rookie Bob Leahy before turning to Bradshaw that day. But when Terry pulled it out, he assured himself a start for the finale.

Terry admitted that he had lost some of his confidence in the second half of the 1971 season. Yet he knew where he wanted to go as a quarterback.

"I've got to learn to control the ball better," he said. "That's the first thing. Then I've got to cut down on the interceptions. And, finally, I've got to start coming up with the big play on more occasions. When I sit back and evaluate this season, I'll see how far I've come to attaining these goals. If I feel I've made progress, I'll be satisfied. I certainly wasn't satisfied with my first year."

There was one final disappointment. The Rams were simply too tough for the young Steelers. Los Angeles jumped to a quick 13-0 lead in the first quarter, and Terry had to play catch-up football. He tossed a three-yard TD pass to tight end Larry Brown in the second period, and a two-yarder to Shanklin in the third. But he also threw four more interceptions, and the Rams won, 23-14.

So another year had ended. The Steelers were 6-8, and Terry Bradshaw was still no superstar, though his 1971 season marked a vast improvement over 1970. He had thrown the ball 373 times, completing 203 for 2,259 yards. His passing percentage was up to 54.4. On the other hand, he threw for just 13 touchdowns as compared with 22 interceptions. He was the eighth-ranking passer in the AFC.

Terry gave much of the credit for his improvement to new quarterback coach Babe Parilli. "The man taught me so much," said Bradshaw. "He taught me things about football I didn't even know existed. He made me into a quarterback instead of just a thrower. I think the statistics speak for themselves."

Parilli gave the praise right back. "Joe Namath is a great quarterback," said the Kentucky Babe, who once played behind Broadway Joe. "And Terry Bradshaw is going to be a great quarterback. Joe can't set up to pass any quicker than Terry. And his arm is as good as anyone's, anywhere. All he needs now is more experience.

"At the end of last season he was starting to realize that he could gain as much yardage with a short pass, rather than a long bomb. His receivers are the ones who can cover the ground. But his playcalling improved and he got away from the hit-or-miss tendencies of his rookie year."

The Steelers looked to be a much-improved club in 1972. The defense was quickly evolving into a crack unit. Flanker Frank Lewis, a second-year man from Grambling, and rookie fullback Franco Harris of Penn State, were giving the team a big lift on offense. Kicker Roy Gerela had one of the better toes in the league. This time all the pressure wasn't on Terry.

Pittsburgh had a tough opponent in the opener, the brutal Oakland Raiders, a team whose defense had been chewing up quarterbacks for years. But this time Terry Bradshaw was ready for them.

In the first quarter, Pitt linebacker Henry Davis gave his club a big boost by blocking a punt, grabbing the ball, and carrying it into the end zone. Minutes later, another young linebacker, Jack Ham, intercepted an Oakland pass. Terry moved the club to the Raider 21, then bolted up the middle on a surprise keeper play and blasted through the Oakland secondary all the way to paydirt. It was a 14-0 game.

Oakland rallied for a score, then Bradshaw brought his team into position for two Gerela field goals. Another march produced Terry's second TD as he scored on a three-yard plunge. The score was 27-7. But then the Raiders came back to score 21 fourth-quarter points and take the lead, 28-27. It looked like the old Steelers again.

Only this time Bradshaw kept his cool. With the ball on his own 43, he dropped back, stayed in the pocket, and lofted a long pass in the direction of Ron Shanklin. The fleet receiver grabbed it near the goal line and went in untouched to complete the 57-yard play. The Raiders held on to win it, 34-28. Terry had completed just seven of 17 passes, but he hit when it counted, ran beautifully, and kept control of the game. For his efforts, he was named Associated Press Player of the Week.

Terry was modest, claiming he didn't deserve the honor, but it boosted his confidence nevertheless. He needed it. The next week the club was beaten by Cincinnati, 15-10. There were several questionable calls, however. Terry threw one TD pass to Shanklin that was called back, and connected with another long one that would have had the club knocking on the door. But the officials ruled that Shanklin was out of bounds when he caught it. Later, a Gerela field goal was blocked. The Steeler defense hadn't been bad. Cincinnati got all its points on five field goals by Horst Muhlmann.

Somehow, it wasn't a typical loss, and the club rebounded quickly to defeat St. Louis, 25-19. The next week, Dallas whipped Pittsburgh in another close one, 17-13, and suddenly the season had reached an early turning point. But there was another event that was to greatly alter the course of the year. Strangely enough, it had nothing to do with Terry Bradshaw.

In the Dallas game, fullback Preston Pearson sustained a serious injury, and rookie Franco Harris was installed in his place. The next week Pittsburgh beat Houston, 24-7, as Harris rambled for more than 100 yards. Three more big wins followed, against New England, Buffalo, and Cincinnati. In each game, the 6-2, 230-pound Harris ran wild, going over the century mark and evoking comparisons with the great Jim Brown. He gave the Steelers the big running game they'd always lacked, and helped take even more of the pressure off Terry.

The Steelers were 6-2 and in contention for the Central Division title in the AFC. And Steeler fans, who had focused on Terry for two years, were discovering other heroes—Harris for one. Franco had a black American father and an Italian mother. Suddenly, Italian-American fans of the Steelers formed "Franco's Italian Army," sat together with banners, and rooted for the big running back.

Another group of fans were taken by the sensational soccer-style kicks of Gerela, and they formed a rooting section called "Gerela's Gorillas." Not to be outdone, some Slovak fans rooted for "Dobre Shunka," the "Great Ham," in honor of linebacker Jack Ham who was having an all-pro season. The Steelers had an identity now, and with the pressure off, Terry could just go out and run the football team.

After beating Kansas City, the Steelers were upset by Cleveland, 26-24, to throw the divisional race into a two-team affair. A win over the Vikings seemed almost routine, as all the Steelers looked forward to the rematch with the Browns. The winner would likely take the title.

The game was played in Pittsburgh on December 3, and more than 55,000 fans came out to cheer their beloved team. The Steelers hadn't won in 40 years of NFL competition. Now the whole town was wild.

Cleveland took the opening kickoff. But four plays later Bo Scott fumbled and linebacker Andy Russell recovered it. Bradshaw came on, and moved the team to the 29. Then Gerela booted a perfect 36-yard field goal. Gerela's Gorillas went wild, as did the rest of the fans, and Pittsburgh was on the scoreboard at 3-0.

Harris ran for a touchdown early in the second quarter to make it a 10-0 game. Meanwhile, the Steeler defense was completely blanketing Mike Phipps and the Browns.

It stayed 10-0 into the third quarter. That's when Ham got into the act, intercepting a Phipps pass and running it to the Browns' six. After an exchange of fumbles, Harris scored his second touchdown and it was 17-0. A few minutes later, Terry reminded fans about his throwing arm, winging a 78-yard TD pass to Lewis. Gerela added another pair of field goals, and Pittsburgh won the ballgame, 30-0.

Two weeks later, the Steelers closed with a 24-2 victory over San Diego, and had themselves an 11-3 season, a divisional title, and a trip to the NFL playoffs.

The year's sensational performances by so many of the Steeler players took Terry out of the limelight for the first time in his career. Franco Harris was great all year. He had gained 100 or more yards in six straight games and finished fourth in the AFC with 1,055 yards on just 188 carries. His 5.6 average per carry was among the best in the league. Gerela finished second to the Jets' Bobby Howfield in scoring with 119 points, making good on 28 of 41 field goal attempts.

As for Terry, he had a steady, albeit unspectacular season. But he was still the engineer of the 11-3 mark, and that couldn't be ignored. Statistically, he completed 147 of 308 passes for 1,887 yards and 12 touchdowns. He wasn't throwing as much because of the powerful running attack. His percentage was just 47.7 but he reduced his interceptions to 12, and that had to be a big plus.

With the newly effective zone defenses, many teams were throwing more to their tight ends, and that was a weak point in the Pittsburgh offense. Shanklin was the leading receiver with 38 catches. It wasn't yet an all-pro year for Bradshaw, but it was surely his most consistent since coming up.

"I think I've matured both on and off the field," he told reporters. "My biggest adjustment has been learning to read defenses, but I feel I've made good progress and will continue to make progress."

One Pittsburgh newsman who had covered the team since Bradshaw came had this to say. "Terry Bradshaw had a good season. The development of some of the club's younger players took the pressure off him and also took him out of the spotlight. That was good. He still hadn't proved himself a super quarterback, but he gave the team what it needed to win and once again showed his tremendous potential."

In the opening round of the playoffs, the Steelers had to face powerful Oakland. They remembered their opening-day 34-28 win against the Raiders, but so did the Raider players. Said fullback Marv Hubbard: "Nobody has beaten us twice in a row. Some teams in our division beat us, but when we played them again, we got even."

The game was played at Pittsburgh on December 23. It will go down as one of the best and strangest games in NFL annals. The two teams were similarly matched, with strong defenses on both sides. For the first half, it was just that, an epic defensive battle, neither team able to score. It began to look as if neither team would break the ice. Oakland's Daryle Lamonica wasn't throwing well, the Pittsburgh line contained their running game. Bradshaw was doing better, but his receiving corps was depleted by the loss of Lewis to an injury, so the Raider defense was keeping them honest.

Midway through the third period, Terry led a drive downfield that stalled at the 11. Gerela came on and booted an 18-yard field goal. The Steelers were on the scoreboard. In the fourth period, it happened again, this time Gerela hitting from the 29. It was 6-0, with the game entering the final session and the Pittsburgh fans beginning to taste victory.

Then Raider coach John Madden made a move. He installed young Ken Stabler at quarterback. Stabler began moving the team, and with about a minute and a half left, he had his club at the Pittsburgh 30. Stabler faded to pass, saw his receivers covered, and took off. Suddenly, he had a wall of blockers in front of him and he streaked down the sideline toward paydirt. The Steeler crowd couldn't believe it as the young QB ran into the end zone for a score. The kick by ancient George Blanda put the Raiders on top, 7-6, for the first time. There was just a minute and thirteen seconds left.

The kickoff went out of the end zone and the Steelers had it at the 20. Bradshaw had to move the team at least close enough for Gerela to have a shot at a three-pointer.

It was no secret that Terry would have to throw. That he did, dropping back five straight times. Two were broken up by free safety Jack Tatum, and two connected with receivers, bringing the ball to the 40-yard line of Pitt. There were five seconds left when Terry Bradshaw faded back to throw his final pass.

The original play called for Terry to throw to reserve wide receiver Barry Pearson. But Pearson was covered. Instead, Terry threw over the middle toward halfback John Fuqua. Fuqua was covered by one defender and Tatum rushed up to bat away the ball. It descended into the maze of bodies, then deflected backwards about seven yards. For a split second all action stopped. It looked as if the game was over.

Then there was movement. Franco Harris was streaking toward the Raider goal line with the football. One Oakland defender took up the chase, but it was too late. Harris rambled the remaining 40 or so yards to complete . . . to complete what? For a minute, no one knew what had happened.

Gradually, it became clear. The football had deflected off Tatum's chest. Since Fuqua hadn't touched it, the ball was still in play. Harris, who was actually not involved in the original pattern, suddenly saw the pigskin coming at him. Instinctively, he grabbed it and took off. By the time the startled Raiders recovered, Harris had gone all the way in. The play was legal. The Steelers had won the ballgame, 13-7.

The play was viewed time and again on replay to erase any doubts about its legality. But the Steelers had won. Terry had completed 11 of 25 for 144 yards, but he was helped immensely by the final turnabout, and refused to take any credit for what happened. Now Pittsburgh would meet unbeaten Miami for the AFC crown. There was no time to rest on any laurels.

There was plenty of pre-game publicity during the week, focusing on the Dolphins' 15-game winning streak, and the powerful young Steelers. Then on Thursday, word came out of Pittsburgh that Terry Bradshaw was in the hospital, knocked out by a 24-hour virus, a strength-sapping ailment that can leave the victim weak and unsteady.

"I'll be ready by game time," Terry told the press. "You can bet on it. I'm just here to rest and get my strength back. One thing I've got is plenty of time to think about Miami."

Once more the Steelers had the home field advantage, and their fans swarmed all over Three Rivers Stadium. Terry was on the field looking no worse for wear and he started the game. Midway through the first period he had his club driving. With the ball at the three, Terry carried around left end. He was hit hard at the goal line and fumbled the ball, but tackle Gerry Mullins fell on it for a Steeler touchdown. It gave Pittsburgh a 7-0 lead, but Terry was shaken up on the play.

Still, Pittsburgh was dominating. Midway through the second period they held Miami again and Larry Seiple dropped back to punt at his own 38-yard line. He took the snap, started his motion—then suddenly took off and ran. The Steelers were caught napping and Seiple carried the ball 50 yards down to the Pittsburgh 12. It was a turning point. Two plays later Earl Morrall passed to Larry Csonka for the score.

On the Steeler side, there was another change. Bradshaw was still woozy from being hit at the goal line and Hanratty was running the team. He couldn't move it. Gerela booted a 14-yard field goal in the third period, but Miami came right back on a Griese-to-Warfield pass for 52 yards. A short run by Jim Kiick made the score 14-10 after three periods.

Steeler fans still believed in miracles. But the Dolphins were now controlling the game. They drove down again and scored, Kiick taking it in for a second time. With the score at 21-10, the Steelers were getting desperate. Chuck Noll put Terry Bradshaw back in the game.

Weakened by his illness and by getting racked up, Terry nevertheless went to work. He just started firing the football. Three completed passes brought it to the Miami 12, and a fourth to Al Young gave Pittsburgh a touchdown. It was 21-17, and it looked as if Bradshaw was hot.

But when the Steelers got the ball again, the magic was gone. The Dolphin defense was laying for Terry and two of his final three passes were picked off and Miami won the ballgame.

Terry had played about half the game and completed five of 10 passes for 80 yards. It was a disappointing finish. Mean Joe Greene, the huge tackle, expressed Pittsburgh's sentiments when he said, "We still think we have the best team. They're good, but small mistakes made the difference."

No one put the rap on Bradshaw. He went as far as he could under adverse circumstances. He had been really racked on the goal line play, and having been sick so close to game time must have hurt. But he was now playing with a good young team, full of exciting talent.

"This is the team of the future, no doubt about it," Terry Bradshaw said during the 1972 season. "And it doesn't matter who's quarterbacking them."

That prophecy was proved false in 1973. It did matter. Terry opened the season with another year's experience under his belt. Like many other quarterbacks in today's game, he was throwing fewer passes and trying to emphasize ball control and running. He fired 23 passes in an opening win over Detroit, then was under the 20-attempt mark in victories over Cleveland, Houston, San Diego, and a loss to Cincinnati.

Wins over the Jets and Bengals followed, giving the Pittsburghers a 6-1 mark. In spite of an uninspiring season by fullback Franco Harris, Pitt was living up to pre-season expectations.

There was one problem. In the Bengal game Terry was hurt, a shoulder separation. He'd be out several weeks. With Terry Hanratty and Joe Gilliam running the ballclub, the Steelers managed wins over Washington and Oakland, their defense doing most of the work. Then suddenly things went sour. Denver, Cleveland and Miami whipped them. Terry returned— rusty—for the Miami game. The Steelers lost.

He pulled things together in the final two games, beating Houston and San Francisco. The club was 10-4, same as the Bengals, but settled for the wild-card berth in the playoffs because the Bengals had scored more points in their two meetings.

The playoff games turned into a rout. Oakland was coming on and whipped Pittsburgh, 33-15. The Pitt defense had been hampered by injuries all year and operating at less than full speed.

Terry threw just 180 passes in '73, completing 89 for 1,183 yards and 10 TD's. He was intercepted 15 times. But it was an incomplete year. There was so much promise at the start. The potential on the Steelers is definitely there.

As for Terry Bradshaw, he is still counted on to become one of the best in the game. He's had to overcome many problems in his early years, but fortunately for him, the team has improved as much as he has. Terry's already realized his initial goal. He's helped make the Steelers a winner.

And with all that firepower in the Steel City, it may not be long before Terry Bradshaw and his teammates are playing in the Super Bowl.

JOHN HADL

Without very many people noticing, John Hadl has marched front and center as one of the best quarterbacks in all of professional football.

John Who?

John Hadl, that's who!

Now just a second. Before the screams of protest become deafening let's get something straight. John Hadl is not an overnight sensation, a one-shot wonder who has recently flashed greatness. He's been flashing it for more than a decade, with a durable kind of consistency that isn't found in too many places nowadays. The problem was that John Hadl was always hanging around the back door. In 1973, he was brought to the front door and he barged through it in a matter of weeks.

The problem was simple. Until 1973, John Hadl had spent his entire career with the San Diego Chargers. They were a good team once, in the early days of the American Football League. But the AFL was considered second-rate then, and so were most of its players. When the leagues merged, the Chargers began to fade. They were in the same division with the Kansas City Chiefs and Oakland Raiders, and played perennial bridesmaids to those powerhouse ballclubs.

As for John Hadl, well, he suffered the same problem as his team. In the realm of great quarterbacks there were the old schoolers, the Starrs, Unitas, Jurgensens, Dawsons. Then there was the new breed that came along around the same time as John, the Tarkentons, Brodies, Gabriels, Namaths. Never was John Hadl considered in the same class as these top flingers. Yet whenever someone would ask Joe Namath who he considered the best quarterback in the league, Broadway Joe would say: "Sure, I'll tell you. John Hadl is the best passer in pro football."

Most people thought Joe was playing games, trying to cause controversy and just giving the sportswriters something to write about. In other words, they thought Joe Willie was putting them on.

But he wasn't. Joe is as astute a football man as you can find and he saw something in Hadl that almost no one else saw. Joe realized the kind of club Hadl was playing with, a weak team defensively that almost always saw the quarterback playing catch-up football.

Hadl was also blessed with some super receivers, guys like Lance Alworth and Gary Garrison, and since the Steelers' running game was inferior, he felt compelled to use them. Then, after the 1972 season, everything changed. John Hadl was traded to the Los Angeles Rams!

What a difference a year makes. The Rams had an experienced quarterback in Roman Gabriel, but they traded him away to make room for Hadl. John stepped in and took the Rams from a mediocre 6-7-1 season in '72 to a 12-2 playoff season in '73. And in doing so, he changed the style that had characterized his play for a dozen seasons. He blended in with new coach Chuck Knox's system and used the personnel at his disposal to the utmost. He showed the critics at last. The old AFL signalcaller was as good as any of them.

John Hadl has learned a lot about quarterbacking during his long career. He knows the good and the bad of pro ball and has definite opinions about his trade.

"A quarterback must have the ability to compete," John has said. "By that I mean the ability to stand in there and take a chance on a beating by a Deacon Jones or a Carl Eller until the right time comes to let go of the football. Passing is timing. Period. The most important thing is releasing the ball at exactly the right instant.

"Therefore, accuracy is a matter of guts. The best passers are those with the most guts. If you have what it takes to outwait Deacon Jones, then you're a quarterback.

"Let me give you an example. When I was with the Chargers we ran a play, a 30-yard post pattern in which the receiver was Gary Garrison, one of the best. Gary and I practiced that play hundreds of times. I knew exactly when he was going to break for the post and when to throw the ball. I also knew just how hard to throw and how much arch to put on the ball. But there's a variable and it's in my stomach. The question is whether I'm going to feel the rush so much that I'll release the pass before I should. If I do, it's an incomplete or worse."

No one has ever questioned John Hadl's guts. Yet he was willing to admit that every quarterback, great ones and veterans included, is sometimes affected by the bone-crushing potential of a professional pass rush. Those tackles, ends, and linebackers aren't playing patty-cakes. They're out for blood and it's usually the quarterback's.

John Hadl has played despite some spilled blood. In fact, he has never missed a single game due to injury. The only other quarterback who can make that claim is Fran Tarkenton. Yet Hadl isn't the scrambler Fran is, and hasn't been able to escape the hard-charging linemen as easily. So he's probably taken more blows than Fran the Scram, but he's never been put on the shelf.

Even a riding accident that left him with a fractured skull and multiple injuries couldn't stop him from starting the season a few months later. But he has paid a price for his unstoppability. Besides the relentless cirticism of his San Diego days, John Hadl has another by-product of his nerve-racking profession—a stomach ulcer, which flares up from time to time. Yet he rarely complains and when game day arrives, John is out there and ready to play ball.

John Hadl has often been referred to as Mr. Middle

America. He hails from Kansas, and that's about as middle as you can get. He's never gone in for the flashy lifestyle of, say, Joe Namath. Yet he and Broadway Joe are the best of friends, with John's home a regular stopping place for Namath whenever the Jets are on the coast.

A chunky 6-1, and weighing about 215 pounds, Hadl doesn't look the type to be a modern-day professional quarterback. He has a round, almost cherubic face and a receding hairline which he makes no attempt to hide. He has been described as looking like a local insurance salesman rather than a glamorous athlete, and he couldn't care less.

It's performance that counts, and John has always been ready, willing, and able to give it his all. He has also given his time to many charitable endeavors, all of which led him to being named Pro Football's Man of the Year in 1971, an award given to the top citizen-athlete in the game.

On the field he has thrown for some 16,300-yard games, establishing a score of Charger passing records during his tenure there. He has now passed for close to 30,000 yards and is number six on the all-time list in this department.

At the age of 34 there are no thoughts of retirement. "I love this game and they'll have to cut the uniform off my back," he has said. "I'll play and play until my arm falls off."

That's a statement you might expect from an old-timer, a player from the 1930's or 40's, a hell-for-leather type liking nothing better than to come off the field with his uniform caked with mud, his face bloodied, but his opponent in much worse shape.

In some ways John Hadl is a throwback. In fact, if he played in the good old days he would have been a triple threat back, and probably a 60-minute man who loved defense as much as offense. He did all of that during his college career at Kansas and had some pro teams looking at him as a runner.

But in other ways John is all modern man. He is devoted to his wife and family and constantly thinks about the future and about providing for them. He had several salary squabbles with the Chargers, asked to be traded on one occasion, and played out his option on another. It seemed that he was always involved in some kind of controversy, yet when the season started he was as reliable as the sun. He was always there, even if there were some clouds partially in the way.

Despite his years on the west coast, he has never forgotten his roots.

"I'm from Kansas," he has often said. "That's where I was born and raised. That's where I went to school, and that's where I'm going to live when my playing days are over."

Lawrence, Kansas, to be precise, the town in which he was born on February 15, 1940. John Willard Hadl was the son of Jess Willard Hadl, named after the legendary heavyweight boxing champion who hailed from that state. Like his namesake, Jess Willard Hadl was a fighter, a man who worked hard to give his family the things they needed.

"My father was also born and raised in Lawrence,"

John recalls. "Times were a lot harder then. He left school in the eighth grade to take a job as a mechanic. His family needed the money. He worked all his life for others and I'll always respect him for that. He made sure I stuck it out through high school and college."

John had kind of a Huck Finn boyhood, free from the pressures of the big cities. He played ball, rode horses, hunted and fished, and had an abundance of easy-living fun. He also helped around the home, worked when he was old enough, and learned the things that go into making up a solid citizen, qualities of honesty and loyalty.

As he neared high school age his interest in athletics grew. He played football and baseball in his spare time, enjoying both. He didn't really care where he played and at one time or another played almost every position in both sports.

By the time he reached Lawrence High he was a big, strong kid who knew how to play ball. He was the quarterback, but also played some linebacker and defensive safety, and he loved contact. As a consequence he ran as often as he could. He wasn't a picture passer, but his arm was strong and he connected often enough to convince college scouts that he could throw. When he made All-State in his senior year the scholarship offers began to pour in.

Charismatic coach Bud Wilkinson of the University of Oklahoma made a big pitch for John. He had him down to the campus and tried to convince him that he could be a big star with the Sooners. John was tempted. He liked Wilkinson and the football pro-

gram that had been outlined for him. But the old loy-
alties were too strong. At the last minute he decided
to stay home and play for Jack Mitchell at the University of Kansas.

John entered Kansas in the autumn of 1958. He
started as a triple-threat quarterback for the Jayhawk
freshman team, then graduated to the varsity in 1959.
There's a high level of competition in the Big Eight
Conference but sophomore Hadl was more than equal
to the task. Even then he had a penchant for the big
play.

He split the quarterback chores that year with a
guy named Lee Flachsbarth, and when he wasn't calling signals he was doing all kinds of other things,
like running back kicks, playing defense, and punting.
He also played some halfback and end. He was by
far the most versatile player on the team.

Against Kansas State that year he ran out of the
backfield and took a pass from Flachsbarth in mid-
stride. He faked one defender, straight-armed another, and rambled 71 yards to the end zone. Kansas
won that one, 33-14.

That same year in a game against Syracuse, John
had kickoff return duty. He grabbed the football at
his own three and started upfield, controlling his
speed until his blocking wall formed. Then he darted
past the first wave of Orangemen tacklers and sprinted upfield. Two good fakes and another block really
sprung him. He was off to the races, a 97-yard kick
return that still stands as a school record.

But the burly sophomore wasn't finished. When
Kansas met Texas Christian that year John was

playing in the defensive secondary. TCU was marching and had the ball inside the 15. The TCU quarterback tried to pass for the score, but he didn't count on the quick reactions of John Hadl. John grabbed the pass by darting in front of the receiver, then ran laterally along the two-yard line for about ten yards. He waited for a block, then cut upfield. More blocks formed, John using them perfectly, waiting for the right moment to turn it on.

When it came he was ready. He pushed the TCU quarterback aside and the last defender was behind him. He then huffed and puffed all the way to the end zone, setting another school record, an incredible 98-yard interception return. It was the only Kansas score of the afternoon.

Then against Oklahoma, the school that wanted him so badly, John showed another side of his fine talent. With Kansas backed up inside the five, he punted out of his own end zone. It was a tremendous boot, sailing high and long, and over the head of the Oklahoma safety. It took a good bounce and when it finally rolled dead it had traveled 94 yards from the line of scrimmage. The huge crowd gave the young sophomore a rousing ovation.

John was a devastating punter all year, setting a Kansas mark of 45.6 yards a kick. And he booted 43 times for 1,960 yards. Most pros don't do that well, and John was only a sophomore.

He made the all-conference team that year, as Kansas finished with just a 5-5 mark. However, the next year he had to forget about all those miscellaneous records. Coach Mitchell made him the team's starting quarterback and told him to concentrate on signalcalling.

With Hadl at the helm the Jayhawkers began to win, opening the year with victories over Kansas State and TCU. The team had changed its strategy somewhat from the season before. Flachsbarth had thrown just 27 times, and the versatile Hadl was the leading scorer with eight touchdowns.

Now, John was in control of the offense. He had fine backs in Bert Coan and Curtis McClinton, but often ran the ball himself from the option. But he threw more than his predecessor and completed 50 percent of his passes.

The team finished strong in 1960, winning four of its final five and ending with a 7-2-1 mark. However, the final wins over Colorado and Missouri had to be forfeited later because of an ineligible player.

Nevertheless it was a big year for Hadl. He completed 43 of 87 passes for 566 yards and ran the ball 108 times for 375 yards, giving him a total offense of 941. His name appeared on several all-America teams and the pro scouts began snooping around the Lawrence campus.

John was really settling down. He met and married his wife, Charneil, that year, and planned a career in coaching when his Kansas days ended. But he still had that senior year and a lot of high hopes for the team.

The Kansas press guide that year had glowing things to say about John, recapping his first two years as a Jayhawk. But there was one note, one phrase, that kept the compliments from getting out of hand.

Brilliant though erratic passer it said.

That was true. Coach Mitchell ran his club from the old split-T formation and there just wasn't that much room for passing. The fact that John liked to run made the pass all the more expendable.

"I had a strong arm, that was about all," John said. "I really didn't know about a passing game and didn't have good control over what I was doing. I threw any way the play dictated, side arm, three-quarters, or over hand. I don't think I delivered the ball the same way twice. It didn't spiral much, but it usually got there. I think I had five picked off as a junior and eight as a senior. But that wasn't really too bad."

Kansas had a strong team John's senior year. He was the leader and the best player. The club won seven, lost three, and tied one, capping it off with a 33-7 victory over Rice in the Bluebonnet Bowl in late December. John was 51 for 103 passing, right around 50 percent again, this time getting 729 yards for his efforts. He ran for another 318 and ended his college career.

His immediate thoughts then turned to his family and his future as a coach, preferably as close to Lawrence as he could get. John was a homebody, all right, and he had no desire to get out and see the world.

But things were happening in the world, as they always are. In the world of pro football a new league had come into existence in 1960, the American League, and was bidding against the older NFL for the top players coming out of the college ranks. Yet even with the increased number of openings for pros, John and his wife didn't give pro football much of a thought. That didn't matter to the pros. They were thinking about him.

Don Klosterman, now general manager of the Rams, was with the San Diego Chargers. The team had started play in Los Angeles in 1960, won the Western Division crown, but lost to Houston in the first league title game. After the year was over, the club moved to San Diego, and Klosterman was one of the club officials out looking for new talent. One Saturday he pulled into Lawrence and came away impressed with the efforts of John Hadl.

"I'm not even sure what game it was," John says now. "But I recall I was throwing from the pocket that day; it just worked out that way. Anyway, for one of the few times all year I was really zingin' them in."

Klosterman wasn't the only one who saw Hadl. The Detroit Lions of the NFL also had their eyes on the Kansas quarterback and had some definite plans of their own.

When the draft rolled around that December, John learned that he had been the number three choice of the Chargers. That was a surprise. But even more of a surprise was the news that he was the number one choice of the Lions!

"We were dumbstruck," Charneil Hadl recalls. "Neither one of us had the slightest idea that either of the pro leagues were interested in John. The draft was as big a shock to us as to anyone. At first we didn't know what to do."

John had to look at the whole thing very closely.

And he had to start from scratch. Since he hadn't thought much about pro ball he hadn't done any homework. Now he had to weigh the two leagues, what they had to offer, and how each might affect his future.

When he started talking with Detroit he learned a curious thing. "They didn't want me as a quarterback," he says. "For some reason or other they figured I'd be another Paul Hornung."

Hornung, of course, was an all-America quarterback at Notre Dame in the late 50's. When he came to the Green Bay Packers he found he couldn't cut it at that position in the NFL. He was almost set to call it quits when the late Vince Lombardi hit upon the bright idea of making Hornung a halfback. There, the Pack took advantage of his multiple talents, utilizing him as a runner, an option passer, and placekicker. For some reason Detroit saw the same qualities in John Hadl. As a matter of fact, it was some good reason.

John was about the same size as Hornung, and seemed to be a good passer, but not good enough to be a full-time QB. He was also a fine punter and smart ballplayer. Thus, another Hornung.

"Not in your life," scoffs John today. "With my dazzling speed. How the heck could I be another Paul Hornung?"

He was kidding, of course. No one will ever know. Perhaps John could have made an all-purpose halfback. He credits his durability to the fact that he played some halfback in college and learned how to take a blow. But he couldn't see himself filling that role back in 1961. So he eliminated the Lions. He didn't want to be cut while trying to be another Paul Hornung.

The Chargers were a different story. They were a new team in a new league looking for young players. He might find a home there. The Charger quarterback was Jack Kemp, a youngster who had been cut by an NFL team, but had played well for San Diego in 1960 and '61. John reasoned he could learn a lot from Kemp, see some action, and perhaps challenge Kemp for the starting post in a year or two. He decided to sign with the Chargers and stake his future on the fledgling American League.

Before reporting to the Charger camp John checked into Chicago to play in the College All-Star game against the NFL champion Green Bay Packers. The Packers won the game, 42-20, but John played well, so well that he was named the All-Stars' Most Valuable Player, becoming the first collegian to win that award in both the East-West and All-Star games.

He didn't have a great game statistically, but he was a natural leader and it showed. He called a cool, competent ballgame. His passing wasn't great, but he threw the ball well enough for the Chargers to like what they saw.

San Diego was coming off a 12-2 campaign in 1961. They won the Western Division title for the second straight year, but lost a 10-3 squeaker to Houston for the league championship. Still, John figured he was reporting to a top team and was looking forward to his rookie year with great anticipation.

Most rookies remember their first day at a pro camp. For John Hadl, it was a day he'd like to forget.

"They had this passing drill with all the quarterbacks taking turns throwing the ball," he recalls. "I just tried to lay it in there real easy and suddenly the whole thing became a nightmare. I couldn't throw a spiral. No matter what I tried the ball kept wobbling and quacking. I was throwing ducks!

"I looked around and everyone was looking at me. I could see the coaches exchanging glances, like they were wondering about this hotshot rookie from Kansas who couldn't even throw a spiral.

"But I somehow threw it off. I was cocky then. I knew I'd make the team and somehow learn to pass better. I wasn't really worried."

John made the team, all right. In fact, as the preseason got underway, a strange thing began happening. Charger players were falling like flies. Kemp was hurt. He'd be out for the year. Star runner Paul Lowe was shelved, also for the season as it turned out. Several other key players found themselves on the sidelines with various kinds of hurts. And as opening day neared, John Hadl suddenly found himself the starting quarterback.

"If someone had told me six months earlier that this was going to happen," John said, "I'd have been willing to bet my life savings against it."

But there it was, opening day at Denver, and starting at quarterback for the defending Western Division champions was number 21, John Hadl.

It was baptism under fire, and John managed to help his team get 21 points on the board. Unfortunately, Denver racked up 30 and won the game. But a week later John turned things around, throwing well and helping his club whip New York, 40-14.

After five games, things were going well. The team was at 3-2 and seemed to be ready to make a run at another divisional title. Then everything seemed to go at once. There were more injuries, the defense wilted, and John made a lot of rookie mistakes. The club lost six straight games and seemed to sink out of sight.

When it all ended, the Chargers had folded to a 4-10 year and dropped to third place in the division. It was demoralizing all around.

"It was rough," John admitted. "I made a lot of mistakes and I know it. But I learned, too. And you can only benefit from this kind of experience."

The experience produced some harrowing statistics. John completed just 107 of 260 passes, and that's just a .412 completion percentage, hardly major league. In fact, the purists just snickered, thinking "typical AFL player—a guy like that couldn't even put on an NFL uniform." But his passes were good for 1,632 yards and 15 touchdowns. That isn't a bad total. The mistakes showed, too. John threw 24 interceptions.

"Hadl was forced to assume an awesome load," said a newsman. "It's bad enough that a rookie is forced to quarterback a team all the way, but when that team is on the brink of a complete collapse, well, that makes it even worse. It's a miracle that Hadl even survived at all. Under the circumstances, I think he did a good job."

And a San Diego assistant coach voiced a similar opinion. "John wasn't ready for full-time duty," the coach said. "He didn't throw that much in college and wasn't really a pass-oriented quarterback. We hoped to bring him along slowly, pick the spots in which he played. Suddenly everything was on his shoulders. But he didn't fold. He hung in there and never quit. We liked him when we picked him and we like him even more now. One good thing about the season was that he learned. He had to. When you put yourself on the line week after week, you learn . . . just to survive if nothing else."

The next year the Chargers regrouped. Coach Sid Gillman didn't like losing and he was determined to put the club together again. He didn't feel he should put the quarterbacking burden on John Hadl altogether. He shopped around for help and came up with a good one, Tobin Rote, a veteran NFLer and proven winner. Rote was in his late 30's and playing in Canada. But Gillman enticed him to come to the AFL and finish his career in San Diego. The wily coach also figured that Rote was just the right man to teach the tricks of quarterbacking to young Hadl. The deal was made in January and Rote immediately became the number one QB.

It didn't really bother John. He knew that Rote had just a year or two left and that the veteran could teach him a lot. He also figured he'd be splitting the QB duties and still getting his game experience. He looked forward to it.

Well, it didn't quite work that way. Rote reported in top shape and quickly showed he was still a top quarterback. He saw the bulk of the action, steadying the young players and providing that all-important experienced leadership. With Paul Lowe back in action teaming with Keith Lincoln, the Chargers had a top running game. And they also had a brilliant young receiver, Lance Alworth of Arkansas, who became an all-league passcatcher in his very first year. From the disaster of 1962 the Chargers roared back, winning five of their first six and jumping back atop the division.

Rote was the main man. John found himself relegated to a total backup role, coming in only when a game was already won or lost. If he had his choice he would have liked to play more, but the club was winning and Rote was doing the job. He really couldn't complain. The club routed Denver in its final game, 58-20, finishing at 11-3 and moving into the AFL title game with the Boston Patriots.

The Chargers had done an amazing turnabout. Halfback Lowe returned and gained 1,010 yards. Rookie Alworth burst on the scene with 61 catches for 1,206 yards and 11 TD's. Rote was an all-league performer with 170 completions in 286 tries, a .594 percentage, 2,510 yards and 20 TD's. That was the kind of offense missing from the 1962 club.

It would have been easy for John Hadl to blame himself for the disaster of the year before. After all, he was the QB then. But John was smart enough to see that other things were different then, as well. In fact, it wasn't surprising in those early days of the AFL for teams to soar up and plummet down in succeeding seasons. The personnel changed rapidly and so did the balance of power. John just happened to be there at the wrong time in his rookie year. He might not have won as many as Rote did in '63, but he didn't have a healthy Lowe or a Lance Alworth, either.

John threw just 64 times in 1963, completing 28 for 502 yards, six touchdowns, and six intercepts. Yet it was still a thrill for him when he warmed up on the Balboa Stadium turf prior to the championship game. A title game is a title game, no matter what the league.

The game was over almost before it began. The first time the Chargers had the ball Rote drove them downfield and ran it over himself from the two. Minutes later Lincoln busted loose on a 67-yard TD run. After the Patriots scored, Paul Lowe came right back by running 58 yards for another TD. It was a 21-7 game at the end of a quarter, 31-10 by halftime.

In the third period Rote fired a 48-yard TD strike to Alworth, making it 38-10, and Coach Gillman figured it was time to let his young quarterback get the taste of championship action.

John came in and played very well. He drove the team to the 25, then dropped back and calmly hit Lincoln over the middle for a touchdown. Late in the final session he led another drive and bulled over from the one to cap the scoring. In a little over one period he connected on six of 10 passes for 112 yards. The Chargers won in a rout, 51-10, and were champions of the AFL.

At the beginning of the 1964 season there were some good signs for the AFL. It was the fifth year of operation and the league seemed to be on steadier ground. Attendance was creeping up and some fine young players (such as Lance Alworth) were spurning the older NFL in favor of the new league. For the first time it was beginning to appear as if the new loop would make it, and talk of an eventual merger with the NFL began to be heard in back rooms and at league meetings.

One sign that the AFL was starting to come of age was in its quarterbacks. During the first three years of its existence, the league featured signalcallers who had at one time or another been in the NFL. They were either veterans like Rote and George Blanda, who had come to the new league to salvage fading careers, or players like 'emp and Len Dawson, who had been cut from the NFL without really having a chance. Dawson, for instance, is recognized as a great quarterback today. Yet if it weren't for the AFL, he might never had gotten a real chance.

At any rate, for the first time the league was starting to scatter its own "home-grown" quarterbacks around, a sign that the league was stabilizing. One sportswriter pointed out that there were some good young ones on the immediate horizon. He pointed to Hadl of San Diego as one with a promising future, saying that he looked about ready to run his own team. Of course, the league was still a year away from its prize catch, Namath of Alabama, but the writer closed by pointing out that the AFL was making progress.

"Some AFL castoffs are even catching on with NFL teams," he said, "and that's a good sign that things are starting to go the other way. But the traffic in quarterbacks is still in one direction, NFL to AFL, and figures to be for some time until the Lamonicas and Hadls take over as first stringers. And when it finally reverses, when an ex-AFL signalcaller starts in the NFL, the new league will really be able to say it has arrived."

Of course the eventual merger changed all that. But in San Diego Sid Gillman was thinking along the same lines. He felt that John Hadl was just about ready and planned to work him into his '64 lineup on a more regular basis.

He did. John split the early games with Rote. That way there wasn't any real pressure on him as he learned and progressed. He was definitely playing better, and when Rote was sidelined with a series of minor hurts, John stepped in and played almost all the way during the entire second half of the campaign.

This time he came through, leading the Chargers to an 8-5-1 mark and another divisional title. The season was tempered somewhat by the fact the team lost three of its final four games, but they had things pretty much wrapped up by then.

John's numbers reflected his progress. He threw the football 274 times in 1964, completing 147 for a 53.6 percentage, good for 2,157 yards and 18 touchdowns. He was intercepted just 15 times. Lance Alworth quickly became his favorite receiver, grabbing another 61 passes for 1,235 yards and 13 touchdowns. He was as good as any flanker in either league.

In the title game that year the Chargers had to face the Buffalo Bills, led by ex-Charger Jack Kemp. Here Gillman had a decision to make and he opted for experience. He decided to start Tobin Rote. The move hurt John, but he accepted it. Rote was on the brink of retiring and John was only in his third year. That made the situation tolerable. Still, it damaged his pride.

The title game hurt everyone. Things went wrong as regularly as they had gone right the year before. For instance, Keith Lincoln ran for 67 yards in the opening quarter of the '63 game. This time he was hit so hard by linebacker Mike Stratton that he was put out of the game.

San Diego managed a 7-3 lead in the opening period, but the Bills made it 13-7 by halftime. After intermission, the Charger offense continued to stall. Rote was just 10 of 26 passing, and Gillman finally turned to Hadl in the final period. John was playing catch up and couldn't do it. The Bills scored again in the final session making it 20-7 and that's the way it ended. John was just three of 10 for 31 yards. It was a disappointing finish to what had been a satisfying season.

In the off-season Tobin Rote officially announced his retirement and Gillman followed that by confirming that he'd now go all the way with John Hadl.

"We're not in the market for a quarterback," the coach said. "We feel we have a good one in John Hadl. He's got the potential to be one of the best and he's definitely our number one man for 1965."

When John reported to training camp he felt good and secure about his new position, and he talked freely about the things he learned and the things he had to do.

"This is the first year I really feel I can do the job, the whole job," he said. "That whole bit about experience is really true. I feel now that I can get out of problems at the line after I see the defense get set.

"I've spent the last three weeks or so going over things with the coaches and I know I'm the number one quarterback. I feel comfortable in the job but I know I've got to produce to stay where I am."

Then John mentioned some of the feelings from his first three seasons.

"At first everything was strange to me," he admitted. "When I came here I felt as if I was starting all over, learning a completely new game. Then I had to wait for an opportunity to play.

"Finally, when I got to play everything seemed confusing. A young quarterback is so concerned with running the game he doesn't have much of a chance to recognize defenses. Now I'm seeing the defenses and the job doesn't appear quite so complicated.

"With Tobin gone I have more responsibility. It's a difficult job, but I like it. The quarterback either gets strong praise or criticism. I've learned to expect it. If a man is going to be well paid he has to take the responsibility. Just knowing I'm number one is good enough for me. Now I've got to produce to stay there."

John produced. He got the team out of the gate fast, throwing and hitting with increasing frequency. Alworth and Paul Lowe were again having banner years and the club won four of its first five, tying the other one.

Then in early November John starting feeling lousy, losing both strength and weight. He went to the hospital for a checkup and was surprised to learn that he was suffering from a stomach ulcer . . . at age 25! Was it the rigors of the profession? Hard to say.

"The diagnosis surprised me," said John. "I always thought I was an easygoing type, at least that's what everyone always told me. Anyway, they put me on a special diet now. No more Mexican food. My weight is down to 205 and the doctor said I might lose some more until I adjust. I can take it to 200, but below that I know I'll lose strength. I guess it's just one of those things that I've got to live with. I can't worry about the ulcer, but I've got to make sure the team keeps winning. You can't help worrying about that."

Coach Gillman reaffirmed his faith in John. "We're still going to win with him," Gillman said. "I have no doubts about that. This thing has been coming on for a while now. John had the flu a few weeks ago and couldn't even talk. Plus his wife was expecting their second child and I know he was worried about her. He's just had a heckuva few weeks."

During the mid-season period when John was down the club dropped three or four. But he started to get his game and his strength back and rallied the Chargers with three great closing weeks, beating New York, 38-7; Houston, 37-26; and Oakland, 24-14. The offensive spurt buoyed the club to a 9-2-3 finish and another Western title.

It was John's best all-around season by far. He threw the ball 348 times, completing 174 for 2,798 yards. That figure was good enough to lead the league. He tossed 20 TD's. His only problem was interceptions. There were 21 of those. But Lowe was an 1,000-yard runner again, and Alworth gained more than 1,600 yards on 69 receptions, including 14 for

TD's. The Hadl-Alworth passing combo was the best in the league.

In the title game that year, the Chargers faced Buffalo once more. The Bills had become the most feared defensive team in the league.

It was scoreless in the first period. Then Jack Kemp tossed an 18-yard TD pass to put his club on top. Minutes later safetyman Butch Byrd picked off one of John's passes to Alworth and returned it 74 big yards for another score. That play seemed to take the heart right out of the San Diego offense. The Bills dominated the rest of the way and won it, 23-0.

John was disappointed again. Playing catch-up ball, he completed just 11 of 23 for 140 yards. He thought to himself after the game that the club would be back, that he'd have another chance soon.

He wanted it, all right, because the structure of pro ball was changing. The NFL and AFL had completed pre-merger plans and were instituting a new championship game beginning after the 1966 season. It was to be called the Super Bowl and would pit the winners from the two leagues against one another for the world championship. How John wanted the Chargers to be the first AFL team to get there!

But it wasn't to be. Nor were the Chargers to make it on their second, third or fourth tries. San Diego was a winner again during the next four years, compiling team records of 7-6-1, 8-5-1, 9-5, and 8-6. The problem was that the Chargers were in the same division with the Kansas City Chiefs and Oakland Raiders. Both those teams were becoming powerhouses. In fact they have dominated the division ever since 1966. Despite those winning years, the Chargers could finish no better than third each time.

In a sense, that's when John began to fall into a kind of groove, a groove of mediocrity. Because the team didn't excel, few people really noticed the outstanding passer who was their leader.

He had a pair of 3,000-yard seasons in 1967 and '68, leading the league in several categories. Unfortunately, the Charger ground game had slipped and John was forced to pass more than he would have liked. He also had to play in many wide-open, high-scoring games, and his interception rate was always up there. For instance, when he fired a league-leading 27 TD passes in 1968, he also threw 32 interceptions, and that figure received more publicity than anything else.

No, not many people said that John Hadl was a great one in those years. Only a few of his peers, men like Namath, told outsiders they were missing the boat on Hadl, that he was a lot better than generally thought. He was getting more publicity for his off-field problems with the Chargers than his on-field performance.

In 1966 some people began to claim that Hadl wasn't really a top pro, that he couldn't win the big ones because of his recent title-game failures.

"For some reason I feel the criticism goes back to the fact that I was more of a runner in college," he said. "That's led to a feeling that I'm an erratic passer, but I'm proving every year that it's not true. I don't care about all-star teams or honors, I'm just bothered when we don't win.

"As for those title games, heck, we just got beat up all around. It wasn't just me, it was everyone. Maybe I didn't play that well, but I don't feel it was a matter of pressure getting me. I didn't feel any.

"You know, it takes a good few years for a quarterback to learn all the things he has to know. I don't feel I had the experience or total know-how until the 1965 season. Now I don't have as much to pick up as I've had in the past. I can concentrate more on finesse like John Unitas, pumping my arm one way and throwing another, or looking one way and firing the other way."

But still another set of critics surfaced and claimed that John wouldn't even have the statistics if it weren't for the inherent greatness of his wide receiver, Lance Alworth. To this, Alworth replied quickly and angrily.

"One of these days people are going to realize that John Hadl is a great quarterback," said Alworth. "I've been saying it all along. He's the most underrated guy in the game. Sure, it takes five or six years to make a good quarterback, but John has gone beyond that. He's tremendous. He does a fantastic job of picking up coverages."

In January of 1967 Hadl clashed with Sid Gillman for the first time. The coach had apparently been harping on some mistakes John had made, especially his high number of interceptions. John felt that some of the remarks indicated a lack of confidence. Finally he barked that he wanted to be traded.

"I owe a lot to Sid," John said. "He taught me most of what I know about the game, but if he's not happy then I'm not happy and it's best we part. I had the feeling that when he used Tensi (a young Charger quarterback) last year he was hoping he'd win the job."

But the storm clouds finally cleared. Gillman wasn't about to trade away the man he'd been grooming for five years and all the experience that went with it. When the 1967 season opened Hadl was still at the helm.

In fact, two weeks before the season started Gillman shipped backup QB Tensi to Denver, further showing his confidence in John.

Game five that year was a great one, a big 45-31 victory over Kansas City, giving the Chargers a 4-0-1. John played control football, grinding out a 24-14 lead while going to Alworth just once.

"See what I mean," Lance said. "John didn't even use me in the first half and called a superb game. I wanted the ball on several third down plays but John knew he'd be throwing to their coverage and he went elsewhere. That's the mark of a real pro."

The real pro completed 17 of 32 passes that afternoon for 307 yards and two TD's. While the team was going well in those early games John threw just three intercepts in five games, the least in the league. It was later, when the defense went sour and John was always trying to catch up, that his intercept total mounted. He finished 1967 with 22, but looking closely at the situation, you can't really fault him. He was to prove it later with the Rams.

In 1968 it was more of the same, just a few key victories short of the playoffs. But Gillman defended his quarterback.

"John has become a great quarterback," said the coach. "Nobody in this game knows as much about it as he does; nothing will ever develop in a game that will shake him up. He may have an occasional bad day. They all do. But he has really grown up. I don't think he'll ever put the ball in the air when he shouldn't."

Yet the trouble wasn't over. John hadn't signed a contract in 1968, and when April of '69 arrived, he was on the brink of playing out his option, the first major quarterback to do so. Word had it that John was requesting a sizable loan from the club for a personal investment. The Chargers refused. That led to an exchange between John and owner Gene Klein, during which Klein supposedly said that John was no Joe Namath, not by any stretch of the imagination.

John said he couldn't play for people who had that kind of attitude and became a free agent. But once again cooler heads prevailed. Before John could sign with anyone else he inked a new four-year pact with the Chargers. He was still their quarterback.

By 1970 the team was fading. Many of the veterans were going downhill, and the youngsters weren't doing the job fast enough. Alworth was injured and dissatisfied himself. But John kept plugging away. Midway through the year Gillman was felled by an ulcer and replaced by Charlie Waller. There was talk of young Marty Domres replacing John at the controls. Then Hadl had a brilliant game against the Bears and was named Associated Press Offensive Player of the Week.

The Chargers had their first losing season since

John's rookie year in 1970, finishing at 5-6-3, but he didn't panic, throwing 22 TD's against just 15 intercepts. Yet it was discouraging. The club seemed to be declining, getting further away from that elusive title instead of closer. Then in the off-season, in March of 1971, something happened to test the mettle of John Hadl again.

What real Kansan wouldn't spend a lot of time on a horse? John always loved to ride and on the afternoon of March 27, he was out riding with his wife Charniel, teammate Steve DeLong and his wife.

John started to gallop past the others when his saddle suddenly broke loose and his was thrown. His head struck a log and he was knocked unconscious.

"It was a horrible sight," said Charneil Hadl. "There was blood coming from his eyes and ears, and he swallowed his tongue. I was in a state of terror."

Fortunately, teammate DeLong didn't hesitate. He rushed to John and pulled out his tongue, a move that may have saved his life. At the hospital, they learned that John was really banged up. He had a fractured skull, a fracture of the orbit of his left eye, and multiple bruises. Dr. Paul Woodward operated on John to correct the eye condition, saying that his vision wouldn't be impaired. There was speculation as to whether Hadl would play at all in '71.

"Don't count John out," said his wife. "He's a strong man. In fact, I don't think someone who wasn't as strong and used to contact could have taken the blow he took."

It was during the recovery period that John realized all over again just how much football meant to him.

"They'll have to tear that uniform off my back someday," he said. "I know how much I love the game. I like everything about it, the waking up on a game day, the feeling of getting suited up, of being taped. I love the tension that builds inside. Then there's the feeling of unity, of the guys being together for one thing ... to win. And I like being the leader of those guys."

There was another new four-year contract for John that spring as he made a complete and rapid recovery and was back running the team by the pre-season. But it wasn't an easy year. The Chargers weren't in good shape, lacking balance and depth, and John had to work very hard. In fact, he found himself taking the blame for several key losses.

He had a brilliant day against Oakland, completing 20 of 35 passes for 321 yards. The Raiders were up by three but the Chargers were driving. Just when it looked as though they might pull it out John fired for the end zone and the ball was picked off.

"I blew it," he said. "The loss is no one's fault but mine. We came back and had them set up for the kill. Then I threw it away."

There was another game with the Jets that saw San Diego trailing by three and driving. On a fourth-down play in the final minute with his team inside the 10, John threw a perfect pass to rookie Ken Dyer in the end zone. The first-year player dropped it, and the Chargers lost.

Another quarterback might have groused about the

rookie, claiming he was robbed of the glory and another TD pass. Not John Hadl.

"It was my fault," he said, as he left the field. "I should have known better. He's just a rookie, a kid, and in a pressure situation I shouldn't have gone to him. It was my fault."

Not many quarterbacks would be big enough to say something like that. Despite a 6-8 campaign John was brilliant in '71. He completed 233 of 431 passes for 3,075 yards and 21 TD passes. All those figures led the conference. He threw for a .541 percentage and had his performance marred by 25 intercepts. But, again, having to play wide-open football in catch-up games didn't help.

The following January John received an honor that he will never forget. He was named Pro Football's Man of the Year, cited for his work as a citizen-athlete. There was a $25,000 scholarship fund set up in the San Diego area in his name.

John won the award for his work with children's hospitals in San Diego, with youth and church groups, and with the Pauma Valley Indian Reservation Development Program. New Charger coach Harland Svare gave him high praise.

"John is as fine a person as you'll find," Svare said. "He fully deserves the honor. It's a great thing for him and our city."

Among the congratulations was a letter from Ethel Kennedy, the widow of Senator Robert F. Kennedy. It read in part:

"... I also really want to thank you for the active interest you've taken in improving the lives of Indians. Dennis McGee, the Robert F. Kennedy Fellow in your area told me of your work in general with the Indians and in particular of the offer of two scholarships to them.

"You're our man of the year in more ways than one."

In 1972 John passed the 25,000-yard mark in passing, becoming the ninth quarterback in the history of the game to do so. But things weren't going well. The Chargers had finally fallen apart. Plus John was having a dispute with Bob Schnelker, the offensive coach under Harland Svare.

"I've enjoyed working with John," Schnelker was quoted as saying. "But we do have different philosophies. I can't change the habits of 10 years of pro football in three months. John has been fighting me all the way."

Schnelker said he wanted a running game and ball control offense with passing as secondary. John didn't say much. He claimed he had a tough time adjusting to a new system. But he also didn't feel the Chargers had the personnel to do it Schnelker's way. And the 4-9-1 record compiled by the team couldn't be blamed on John. He didn't have a bad year considering the club.

But this was one storm that John and the Chargers couldn't ride out together. It was understood that the time had come for a parting of the ways. In January, the move came. The first step was a strange one. The Chargers were supposed to be rebuilding, but they acquired the contract of the great John Unitas from the Colts. The problem was that Johnny U. was 39 and oft-injured. Yet once they had him they felt freer about dealing Hadl.

A few days later Svare called John and informed him that he was traded to the Los Angeles Rams for defensive lineman Coy Bacon and running back Bob Thomas. John was overjoyed.

"This is a perfect situation," he said. "I'm very excited about coming to Los Angeles and becoming a Ram. The Rams have the greatest owner in the league in Carroll Rosenbloom, a great guy with a great track record. And Don Klosterman, well he's an old buddy of mine, the guy who made me a Charger draft choice in '62. And I heard that the new coach, Chuck Knox, is a great football man."

John approached his first Ram camp with the enthusiasm of a rookie. The club had fallen off in '72, with a 6-7-1 mark, but still had the nucleus of a good team. Roman Gabriel was the long-time quarterback at L.A., but when he heard Hadl was coming he himself asked to be traded and wound up in Philadelphia. So the door was open for John to take over.

"I've never felt this way about a season before," John said. "It's like being reborn. I'm in the best shape since 1965 and I feel like a rookie all over again."

All the Rams were rookies, in a sense, because they had to learn the new system. Chuck Knox analyzed his personnel and decided how he wanted to play it. When he told John he was striving for a strong running game and powerful defense, the long-time QB agreed. Those who thought John was pass happy didn't really understand his situation on the Chargers.

With the Rams, John had two excellent running backs to work with, Jim Bertlesen and Larry McCutcheon. He also had a true gamebreaker of a pass receiver in little Harold Jackson, who had come over in the Gabriel deal. So John had the tools. Now they were his to work into a winner.

John's Ram career opened on a high note, a 23-13 win over Kansas City. He emphasized the things Knox wanted, the ball control and good running game, and it worked. A big win over Atlanta came next, then San Francisco, Houston, Dallas, and Green Bay fell. The Rams were 6-0 and the surprise team in football.

As for John, he was doing everything right, playing a different kind of game than he had in the past, but it was working. Bertelsen and McCutcheon were tearing up the league on the ground and John didn't have to pass much. But when he did he was accurate and devastating.

Through six games he had completed 60 of 93 passes for 961 yards. That's an amazing 64.5 percent completion. He also had 13 TD passes and just two interceptions. That showed what Hadl could do under the proper conditions.

"Things have changed," Hadl said. "To win in the league now you've got to play consistent defense, maintain control of the ball, and master a flexible passing game. By that I mean you might not pass much but you need things you can count on when you do pass. That's what the Rams are doing.

"Football today is a game of turnovers, field position, and mistakes. The top teams run the ball until they see an opportunity for a quick strike."

The following week the Rams met the Minnesota Vikings, also unbeaten at 6-0. It was an epic battle, veterans Fran Tarkenton and Hadl trying to outfox one another. It was also a tremendous defensive battle and when it ended the Vikes were on top, 10-9.

"I tried everything," said John, "but they just out-executed us. They're the best defensive team we've faced. No matter what we did we couldn't get momentum going."

There was another loss the next week, a 15-13 upset at the hands of Atlanta. But after that Hadl pulled the club together. They started moving again, reeling off six more easy victories to close out the season as divisional champs with a 12-2 log.

It was an amazing turnabout for the Rams. Much of the credit went to Chuck Knox, who remolded the ballclub in one season. And much of the credit went to John Hadl, who changed his style and became all-pro. But there was even more to it than that.

As Hadl said, the modern team needs defense. The Rams had it, giving their opponents just 178 points. And the modern team needs ball control. They had that, too. McCutcheon gained 1,097 yards, Bertelsen 854. And the modern team needs a passing game for the special situations. Well, little Jackson ran for 874 yards on less than 40 passes. That's not all. Thirteen of those passes went for touchdowns.

Then there was the quarterback. Hadl's statistics would surprise many a long-time San Diego fan. They were a whole different kind of number.

John threw the football just 258 times. Since 1965 he had always been over 300 passes; three times he'd been over 400. Anyway, he completed 135 for a 52.3 percentage and 2,008 yards. It was his lowest yardage total since his sophomore year in college. But 22 of his passes went for touchdowns, and that was just one behind the NFL leader. Finally, only 11 of his throws were intercepted, the lowest total of his pro career. Overall, John Hadl was more effective than he had ever been before. And he did it the way many critics said he couldn't, by changing his style.

He became a control quarterback, passing only when he had to. But he kept the other teams honest. Against Dallas early in the year, he fired four TD passes to Jackson, and hit Harold on another long bomb against the 49ers at just the right time. He wasn't about to let the defenses forget that John Hadl was a flinger from way back. But he was also smart enough to realize how the game had changed.

"The zone defenses they play today make interceptions more likely," said John. "Against a man-for-man defense you can throw the ball over your receiver's head if you see him covered. But with the zone, there's always a chance somebody who is slightly out of your line of vision will sneak up there and intercept, even if you're trying to throw the ball away. Because of this, the good teams today throw only when they have to."

But whatever Hadl and the Rams did it worked. Los Angeles was back in the NFL playoffs, and John was in them for the first time. In the first round, L.

A. had to go up against Dallas at the Cowboys' home stadium.

The game was rated just about a tossup. Both clubs were solid defensively and had offenses that could explode. John had the experience edge over the Cowboys Roger Staubach, and many figured this would be a telling factor in the game. But no one counted on the intangibles of pro football, or any sport for that matter—the intangibles that dictate which of two good teams will dominate the other.

Dallas decided to concentrate on two things. They'd defense the Rams running game and make sure Hadl couldn't go long to Jackson. What the Cowboys didn't expect was that their own offense would take off so quickly.

Twice in the opening period the Cowboys drove downfield and scored, first Calvin Hill on a short run, then on a four-yard pass from Staubach to receiver Drew Pearson. That made it 14-0. In the second period Toni Fritsch kicked a 39-yard field goal to make it 17-0, and it looked as if the Rams were done.

But Hadl and his mates didn't quit. John knew he wasn't having a good passing day. The pinpoint precision that a QB can feel wasn't there. Still, John knew he had to move fast once the Cowboys took the lead. Twice before the half ended he engineered determined drives that culminated in David Ray field goals. That made it 17-6.

The third quarter was scoreless, but the Rams had one more move to make. Ray kicked another field goal early in the fourth quarter to make it 17-9. Then the Rams got a break. Calvin Hill fumbled on the 17 and Hadl came on to take his team in, Tony Baker scoring on a five-yard run. Now it was 17-16 and a ballgame.

Dallas got the ball and the Rams were fired up. They threw Roger Staubach for a loss, then batted down a pass. It was third and 14 for Dallas, the ball on their 17. If the Rams could get it back, their momentum might take them right to a victory.

Quarterback Staubach got the call from his coach, Tom Landry. The coach wanted a deep sideline pass to Bob Hayes, the speedy flanker. Staubach called it, but also told his other wide receiver, Pearson, to run a deep post instead of a short curl, which he usually ran on the pass to Hayes.

At the snap, Roger dropped back, saw Hayes covered, and threw in the direction of Pearson. The rookie receiver was between two Ram defenders but somehow he got his hands on the ball, pulled away, and took off. It was an 83-yard touchdown play and it broke the back of the Ram rally. Dallas went on to win, 27-16, and advance to the NFL title game. For the Rams, the season was suddenly over.

"We didn't quit," said Coach Knox. "We came back and almost had them. One play did us in."

All John could say was, "We'll be back." He again took the blame for the defeat upon himself. He had hit on just seven of 23 passes for 133 yards. But in all fairness, there were other Ram breakdowns. The running game produced just 93 yards, and Jackson was blanketed except for one 40-yard catch. In addition, the Ram defense didn't tighten until the second half.

It just wasn't their day, but it couldn't completely take away from a great season.

The whole 12-2 scene was re-emphasized two weeks later when the club learned that John Hadl, their leader and quarterback, had been named Player of the Year in the NFC. It was an honor that had been due for a long time.

"No one deserved it more than John," said Chuck Knox. "He changed habits acquired during a great career in San Diego and led us to a title. I can't think of any other quarterback I'd rather have leading my team."

John didn't say much. It was as if the award, the recognition, was for 12 years and not one. He simply summed up his philosophy of play selection gathered during his long years in the league.

"It takes the ability to come up with plays they don't expect. The way to succeed at quarterback is to call the unexpected consistently."

John Hadl couldn't always do that at San Diego. Too often he had to just drop back and throw in an attempt to bail his team out of a jam. At L. A. he could practice what he preached and everyone came up winners. John has discovered a new life and a new career with a strong team, one that has rebuilt itself well and should stay on top for a long time.

Though John is no youngster, his record of perfect health and a strong arm should keep him going for years more. And the Rams aren't about to tear that uniform off his back.

John Hadl is a great quarterback, all right. Joe Namath, for one, was saying it years ago. It just took everyone else a long time to find out.

Mike Phipps   145

Phipps was in his third season with the Browns, after a record-breaking career at Purdue, but in only

MIKE PHIPPS

It was a Monday night, November 13, 1972, and
the Cleveland Browns were playing the San Diego
Chargers in a nationally televisied NFL game. For
the Browns, it was almost a "must" game. The club
had a 5-3 record and needed another victory to get
back into the Central Division race in the American
Conference. But in the Chargers, the Browns had run
into a more than formidable foe.

With less than two minutes remaining in the game,
San Diego was in the process of completing a touchdown drive that was to give them a 17-14 lead. Suddenly, defeat was staring the Cleveland club squarely
in the face. Young Mike Phipps glanced up at the
clock after the Browns took the San Diego kickoff
back to their own 36-yard line. There was just one
minute and one second left. It was perhaps the biggest pressure situation of Mike Phipps' career.

144

Phipps was in his third season with the Browns, after a record-breaking career at Purdue, but in only his first year as a starter. He didn't feel he yet had command of the team, many of the veterans still feeling that injury-prone Bill Nelsen could do a better job. So young Phipps felt a special kind of pressure as he jogged out onto the San Diego turf. The crowd was chanting DEFENSE, DEFENSE, and the clock was poised and ready to drop below the minute mark. Phipps knew he wouldn't get a second chance.

On the first play he dropped back quickly, waited a second, then threw a short pass over the middle to fullback Ken Brown. It was complete for about eight yards. Second and short yardage. Phipps dropped back again, the San Diego line charging hard, and he calmly threw over the middle once more, again hitting fullback Brown for a first down on the San Diego 38. Then he called a time out and came over to the sideline.

Browns head coach Nick Skorich and veteran Nelsen huddled with Phipps.

"They think we're trying to manuever for a field goal," Nelsen said. "The cornerback is playing Frank (wide receiver Frank Pitts) awfully tight. Why not go for broke on this one? We'll still have time to get closer for a kick."

Skorich said nothing. He'd let his two quarterbacks decide. Phipps sized up the situation. A mistake now would be costly. The Browns had a good kicker in Don Cockroft and it would be safer to try to eat up another 10 or 15 yards and let him boot for the tie. But then again, you can't always play safe. Mike knew that Nelsen was right. He wondered if he had the confidence to pull it off.

"OK, we'll try it," he said. Nelsen smacked him on the rump and Mike jogged back to his teammates. He snapped them together and called the play quickly and authoritatively. No one argued.

Phipps came up to the line and checked over the defense. Sure enough, cornerback Ray Jones was playing up on Pitts, hoping to stop the short posts or squareouts. There'd be no audible, Mike would keep the play. He called signals and took the snap.

Backpedaling quickly, he looked to pick up Pitts. His receiver was streaking down the right side and already had two steps on Jones. Now it was up to Mike to lay it in there. Ignoring the footsteps that were closing in on him he let the ball go in a high, almost lazy arc, the kind of leading pass that if thrown right would come spiraling down just as the receiver ran under it.

Without breaking stride Pitts crossed the goal line, glanced up, and saw the ball coming down over his left shoulder. He simply reached up and caught it, as easy as picking an apple off a tree. It was a perfect play. The Browns had scored.

As he came off the field Phipps' teammates mobbed around him, pumping his hands, smacking his helmet and shoulder pads. It had taken him just 41 seconds to bring his club 64 yards and produce a winning touchdown. It couldn't have been done any better. The Browns had a 21-17 victory, their fourth straight, a 6-3 record, and remained just one game behind Pittsburgh in the divisional race. And they had the momentum they needed for the upcoming game with the Steelers, set for the following week.

"When I came on the field I really felt we were going to score," Mike said after the game. "I wasn't sure it would be a touchdown, but at least a field goal to tie it. To be honest, I wouldn't have called the bomb. We still had 47 seconds left and I think I would have tried to work closer with short passes. But when Bill suggested I try it I felt I should. He's been around a lot longer than I have and knows the game. There's no substitute for experience."

But Phipps was finally getting that experience, after two years of being a backup to the gimpy-kneed Nelsen. Now, he was beginning to acquire two things that are a must for pro quarterbacks—confidence and respect.

"Mike is really coming on," said his receiver, Pitts. "We're all beginning to lean on him more and more. We needed that touchdown badly and he threw one of the most perfect strikes since we began playing together last year.

"Let me tell you something. The guy is pushing and nudging and demanding respect. And once we all get that feeling in our own minds we can go anywhere."

It wasn't always that way for Mike Phipps. He came out of Purdue an all-American. He broke college records set by a couple of guys named Len Dawson and Bob Griese, and that made him pretty special right there. He had the size, 6-3, 205 pounds, and was second in the Heisman Trophy voting his senior year. It looked as if he had it made.

The Cleveland club had a winning reputation matched by few. The team was formed in 1946, joining a maverick league called the All-American Football Conference. For four years, the Browns dominated the AAFC, winning four straight divisional crowns and four AAFC championships. In 1948 the team was 14-0 during the regular season and whipped the Buffalo team, 49-7, in the title game. Not many teams have compiled a record like that.

When the AAFC disbanded in 1949, the Browns were allowed to enter the National Football League, their team intact. Many people figured the Cleveland club would be brought down to earth by the NFL competition, but the Browns took up where they left off, tying the Giants for the Eastern Conference crown with a 10-2 record. Then they beat the Giants in a playoff and whipped the Los Angeles Rams, 30-28, for the NFL championship.

From there, the Browns went on to win five more divisional crowns in a row and two more NFL titles. They've won eight divisional races since then and have always remained close to the top. In other words, the Cleveland Browns have been winners since the very beginning.

Though the team has been in existence for almost 30 years, there have been only a few major quarterbacks. The club picks their leaders carefully and sticks with them for years.

Otto Graham was the first and generally acknowledged as the best. He was a master passer and dynamic leader, and the hero of the team's dramatic entrance into the NFL in the early 1950's. When Graham retired a few interim QB's were tried, then Milt Plum came along in a trade with Detroit. Plum had limitations, but utilized his positive assets very well. He was an effective leader.

Following Plum was Frank Ryan, who led the team to its last world championship in 1964. Ryan was an intelligent, confident passer who could throw long with the best of them. There were again some interim quarterbacks for a couple of more years before Nelsen joined the team in 1968. The Cleveland people figured Bill would be around for quite some time, but he quickly ran into leg problems. And after his third operation it became obvious that he wouldn't be able to play much longer, even though he was not yet 30 years old.

So the team began shopping around again. There were some good ones coming out of the college ranks in 1969, the best reputed to be Louisiana Tech's Terry Bradshaw, Purdue's Mike Phipps, and San Diego State's Dennis Shaw.

Since the Browns had their usual winning team in '69, they'd be pretty low on the draft list, the blue-chip quarterbacks certainly gone by then. So something had to be done. The club thought it out and decided to take a daring gamble. They traded their popular all-pro wide receiver, Paul Warfield, to the Miami Dolphins in return for the number three choice in the upcoming draft. The move was harshly criticized in Cleveland. The result of the move was that the Browns got Phipps. (Bradshaw had gone to Pittsburgh as the first pick.)

That put Mike under tremendous pressure right

from the start. The Cleveland team had also traded with the New York Giants to get wide receiver Homer Jones. They hoped he'd replace Warfield. But Jones sort of disappeared into the background. All the long-time Cleveland fans knew was that Warfield was gone and here was this Phipps kid who caused it to happen. They waited for Mike to produce.

Nelsen held the number one spot in 1970, Mike's rookie year, but at the outset of training camp in '71, Coach Nick Skorich handed the job to Mike and told him it was his as long as he could hold it. He couldn't, giving way to Nelsen by the time the regular season started. Thus, the pressure began to mount.

It was the same situation in '72. Mike flopped miserably in training camp. Though Nelsen's knees were in worse shape than ever he started the opening game. It was beginning to look as if the Browns had come to a dead end with Mike Phipps.

Then Coach Skorich took a gamble. Nelsen was having more trouble than ever moving around in the backfield. Instead of going with Nelsen and throwing Phipps in here and there, not a very stable situation, for the team or for Mike's development, he decided to put Phipps in and stay with him, starting with the second game of the 1972 season.

So that's the way it happened. Mike became the starter and hasn't relinquished the position, earning the respect of his teammates as he continued to learn his trade. And the youngster who first quarterbacked a team when he was six years old finally made it to the big time.

Mike's childhood was spent in Columbus, Indiana, though he was born in the nearby town of Shelbyville on November 19, 1947. Mike was always close to his parents and both of them helped him with his athletic development.

"I liked all the sports," Mike recalls, "though football was always my favorite. When I was just five years old, my mother bought me a football uniform for Christmas. I would wear it constantly. And when I started playing with other kids in the neighborhood I was always the quarterback.

"Even when I was by myself I was thinking about football. I set up my own field in our back yard by putting up a couple of fence posts for goal posts and working on kicking along with everything else. When I'd play with the other kids, I'd always seem to rip my tee shirt. I remember coming home all dirty and banged up, and always with a torn tee shirt. My mom would just look at me and shake her head. She couldn't believe it."

Mike's father was a state policeman in Indiana and he played ball with young Mike whenever he had a chance. He also taught the youngster respect for the law and in turn listened to the problems of youngsters.

"When you're around police as much as I was you begin to have a greater understanding of the problems they face," Mike said. "My father also learned about kids from me. I remember when I got my new car, a Corvette Sting Ray. I took him for a ride and started telling him all about the car. 'Son,' he said, suddenly, 'You can't tell me anything about these things I don't know. I've been chasing them all my life.'"

So Mike's development followed a normal, happy course. There were no pressing problems or excessive pressure. Yet he quickly developed the true athlete's natural hunger and desire to excel and win. He was constantly trying to improve himself and learn new things. His love for the game never waned at all.

"Other sports were great, too," he says, "but football continued to be my favorite. At Columbus High School I started participating in the program when I was in the ninth grade. My first two years there was a quarterback named Rick Stoner who was real good and I only played part time. Then, when I was a junior there was another senior ahead of me but the coach decided to make him a split end and move me in at quarterback. It worked out well for both of us.

"I started my last two years. Things went very well and I found myself setting another goal. I decided I'd love to be a Big Ten quarterback."

Mike became a star at Columbus in the two years he started. He already had a strong arm and passed well. Plus he was big and strong enough to run with the ball. In two years he compiled a total offense of 3,450 yards and completed some 53 percent of his passes. He received numerous scholarship offers and decided to stay in his home state and attend Purdue University. He entered the school in the fall of 1965.

When Mike was playing on the Boilermaker freshman team Bob Griese was a record-setting senior. Mike watched him week after week and was amazed at the way Griese operated on the gridiron.

"I never dreamed I'd be breaking the records I saw him setting," Mike said. "But that's what the game is all about. I'm sure someone will come along someday and break the records I've set at Purdue."

He didn't start setting records right away. As a freshman, he shared the position with several other QB's. And when he reported to his first spring practice in 1966, there were seven other quarterback candidates for Griese's vacated position. Mike wondered if he'd get lost in the shuffle.

"I wasn't doing that well in the spring," he recalls. "My passes were wobbly and erratic and I wasn't throwing the ball right. It was a rough time. I couldn't seem to find my receivers quick enough and didn't know why my passing was so spotty. I figured I was in the process of blowing my chance right then and there."

But head coach Jack Mollenkopf and quarterback coach Bob DeMoss didn't want to rush a decision. The QB job was still up for grabs when the team reported late in the summer for pre-season work. It was soon obvious that a few of the candidates didn't really have what it takes. It became a two-man competition, between Mike and a junior who had seen very limited action the year before.

"When I reported that summer I began having some of the same problems from the previous spring, namely that my passing was erratic and I was unable to locate my receivers quickly enough. But I stayed late after practice and gradually worked it out with the help of the coaches. All of a sudden I seemed to get the overall picture of the defense and things began falling into place."

Then 10 days before the season began the other quarterback, the junior, got a sore arm. He couldn't throw at all and wouldn't until it was time for the opener. So the coaches made their decision right then and there. They'd go with the sophomore, Mike Phipps.

"In a way the decision was made for us," said Bob DeMoss, "but Mike had been coming on anyway. He improved during the spring workouts and kept coming on and standing out in the pre-season. The rest, as they say, is history."

But it was harder for Mike to make that history than it had been for previous Purdue quarterbacks. Bob DeMoss tells why.

"College defenses were becoming more and more complex. It seemed that every year teams were coming up with new and more sophisticated defensive manuevers, so Mike had to learn more than any quarterback we ever had. We threw it all at him pretty fast, but he took it well."

In a way Mike disagrees with his coach. He said they didn't rush him and put undue pressure on him.

"Coach DeMoss was very patient. He gave me the basics as a sophomore and didn't expect me to do the things Bob Griese had done before. He developed our offense according to what I could do and then expanded it as he saw me starting to do other things."

The Boilermakers opened up against Texas A & M at Dallas. Mike had a good supporting cast with tough runners Leroy Keyes and Perry Williams in the backfield. The Aggies scored first on a 22-yard field goal, then Phipps went to work. He wasn't shy about throwing the ball in his first varsity game. He just came out, drove his team downfield, and connected with halfback Vic Baltzell on a 35-yard scoring pass to give his team the lead.

By halftime Mike had thrown for more than 200 yards and Purdue was well on its way to victory. The final was 24-20, with Mike completing 17 of 35 for 259 yards. It was a smashing debut for the youngster and both coaches, Mollenkopf and DeMoss, knew they had made the right choice. But there was another test coming. Texas A & M was just an average opponent. Next week the Boilermakers would be meeting Notre Dame. If Phipps were going to fold, the Irish were the team to force him into it.

Purdue scored first, Mike leading a drive downfield and fullback Williams going over from the 10. The kick missed and Purdue had a 6-0 lead. Then the Irish came back. Their quarterback, Terry Hanratty, was a good one and brought his team downfield before taking it in himself from the one. The kick was good and the Irish had a 7-6 lead which they still held at halftime.

In the third quarter both quarterbacks opened up, especially Hanratty, who was throwing the ball all over the place. Yet it was Mike who got his team in first, Williams scoring again from the three. This time Mike threw for the point, hitting his all-America end, Jim Beirne. That made it 14-7. But before the quarter ended Rocky Bleier scored from the one and the kick tied the game again. It was 14-all going into the final period. Now sophomore Phipps was really under the gun.

Showing a cool usually reserved for hotshot seniors, Mike went to work. He ignored the heavy Notre Dame rush and passed with precision and poise. He drove his team downfield, then hit Keyes with an 11-yard TD toss to give Purdue the lead.

But the see-saw action continued. Hanratty passed 27-yards to Jack Snow and the game was again tied at 21. Then Mike took over for the final assault. It was a real pressure situation. There were just minutes left when he had the team on the 31. The Irish defenders snarled across the line at the youngster, telling him that they were coming hard.

Mike took the snap and dropped back. He looked downfield and quickly picked up halfback Baltzell speeding toward the end zone. The footsteps were closing fast and he released the ball just before being hit hard by two huge linemen.

He was on his back when he heard a roar come up from the 62,000-plus fans at Lafayette. He knew Baltzell had the football. He knew his club was going to win the game!

The final was 28-21, with Mike completing 14 of 34 passes for 238 yards and two scores. His percentage wasn't high, but the yardage total showed he hit the big ones when he had to. By contrast, Hanratty had thrown the amazing total of 63 times, completing 29 for 366 yards. But he was intercepted four times, while Mike had had none picked off, and the telling factor was the seven more points Purdue had put on the scoreboard.

"We knew Mike was the real thing after that Notre Dame game," Bob DeMoss said. "He didn't panic, didn't rattle, didn't try to rush things. When he missed a few passes he didn't press. And even though he completed 14 of 24, none of the 20 misses was picked off. That's saying something, too. Yes, when Mike won that game we knew we wouldn't have to worry about our quarterback situation for the next three years."

Mike improved almost each week. He saw limited duty in two mid-season games because of an ankle injury, and saw his club lose only twice, a 22-14 setback to Oregon State and a season-ending heartbreaker to Indiana, 19-14. That game dropped the Boilermakers into a three-way tie for the Big Ten title with Purdue, Indiana and Minnesota with 6-1 conference marks. The team was 8-2 overall and ranked number nine in the nation.

As for Mike, he did better than anyone imagined. He was setting records already, breaking the Purdue total offense mark with 2,020 yards. He also finished number three in the nation in that category. In passing he completed 118 of 243 for 1,800 yards, and that was more than Dawson, Griese, or any other Purdue quarterback for a single season. He threw for 11 touchdowns and had just seven intercepted, an impressive figure for a sophomore.

There were other honors, too. He was named to the first team of the all-Big Ten squad, and made the second team Academic All-America. He was already a strong B student in Industrial Management.

In the off-season Mike continued to work on improving himself as a player. He also pursued his favorite form of recreation other than football, hunting and fishing around Columbus. When the 1968 season rolled around he was ready to take up just where he left off.

He led his club to an easy 44-6 win over Virginia in the opener, then got set for the rematch with Terry Hanratty and the Irish of Notre Dame. It turned into the same kind of wide-open game as the year before, only this time Phipps and company made sure it wasn't as close.

There was a field goal in the first period, then three TD's in the second, Mike throwing for one of them. It was 23-14 at the half and the final was 37-22. It was a great game for the all-America Keyes, who ran well and even threw an option pass touchdown. Mike was good too, completing 20 of 30 passes for 259 yards.

Purdue had an outstanding team in 1968. The Boilermakers were unbeaten and ranked number one in the country through three games, then lost to Ohio State, 13-0. They won the next one over Wake Forest, but Mike had to leave that game early with a badly sprained ankle, which also caused him to miss the next two contests. He came back against Minnesota only to see his club beaten, 27-13. But he rallied them to win the final two games for another 8-2 year and a national ranking.

Because of the missed time to injury and the powerful running game led by Keyes and Williams, Mike didn't throw as often or pick up as many yards. He was 88 for 169, with only three TD's and nine intercepts. His yardage dropped to 1,096 and his total offense to 1,118 yards. But he still led the club to an outstanding season. The test would come the next year. Many of the outstanding players would be graduating. In fact, Mike and his center were the only returning starters on the offensive unit. Many observers picked the Boilermakers to finish below the .500 mark.

What they didn't count on was a tremendous season from Mike Phipps, one that far surpassed all expectations and not only projected Mike into the thick of the Heisman Trophy race, but made him a blue chip prospect in the following pro draft.

With Keyes and Williams gone, the ground game dissolved into mediocrity. Purdue opponents knew Mike was going to be throwing more and they were ready for it, but they still couldn't stop it.

The team opened with a 42-35 victory over TCU, with Mike giving a preview of what was to come with an 11-for-24 day, producing four touchdowns and 286 yards. The next week he became the only quarterback in Purdue history to engineer three straight victories over Notre Dame. This time the Boilermakers won, 28-14, with Mike completing 12 of 20 for 213 yards.

After that the team met Stanford University and their great quarterback Jim Plunkett. It was a game Purdue fans will never forget.

From the outset it was obvious that the game would be a passing battle between Phipps and Plunkett. The two big quarterbacks came out firing and never stopped. Mike threw three TD passes in the first half alone, hitting from 11, 29, and 25 yards out.

Meanwhile Plunkett had thrown for two and saw his halfback score one on the ground. So at the half it was a 21-21 ballgame.

In the third quarter Stanford began taking over. They were holding the ball and pushing the Boilermakers around. Plunkett, meanwhile, was finding his receivers. He flipped a 10-yard TD pass to Bob Moore, then a nine-yarder to Rick Kadziel, giving his club a 35-21 lead with only a quarter to play. Things looked bleak.

Mike knew he'd have to throw the ball, so did Stanford, but they couldn't stop him. Everything he threw seemed to be finding its mark. He drove his club downfield and from the 21 hit John Bullock in the end zone to bring the team within seven.

This time the Boilermaker defense stopped Plunkett and gave the ball back to Phipps. Mike just went back to throwing, dropping back, confidently looking downfield, and then rifling the ball home. From the 14 he did it again, taking two steps to his right, then hitting halfback Stan Brown over the middle for a touchdown.

There wasn't much time left. Purdue could kick for the point and a tie, or they could run or pass for two points and a win. The coaches decided to go for the victory. Mike came to the line and checked over the Stanford defense. He decided to throw. Taking the snap he rolled to his right, then spotted end Greg Fenner cutting for the corner of the end zone. Once again Mike's pass was on the mark. The conversion was good, and Purdue had won the ballgame, 36-35.

It was a great victory and a tremendous performance by Mike Phipps. Mike had completed 28 of 39 passes for 424 yards and five touchdowns. In the final period alone he had hit on all 12 passes he tried, an amazingly accurate performance, a perfect performance, in fact. He capped it with his clutch conversion pass that gave Stanford the victory. He was the AP Back of the Week and received nationwide publicity for his efforts.

Mike continued his brilliant passing and leadership all year long. Losses to Michigan and Ohio State marred the season but another 8-2 log was more than most people expected when the campaign began.

"You could watch this team come on from nothing," Mike remarked. "Everyone helped. More work went into this team than you can ever imagine and I'm more proud of it than any other I've been on."

Coach DeMoss pointed out that the modest Phipps was always ready to give credit to others. "Mike carried us," said DeMoss. "We put a monkey on his back when it began and he came through. Mike was a leader and an inspiration. He worked to improve every game, every week. Both Len Dawson and Bob Griese were the same way before him. They are players who are never satisfied, and that's the mark of any good athlete."

Statistically, Mike produced a brilliant season. He completed a school record 169 passes in 321 attempts for a .526 percentage and 2,527 yards. He threw for 23 touchdowns and produced a total offense good for 2,745 yards. He established a new Big Ten mark of 1,699 yards total offense for the year.

He also became the first Boilermaker to gain more

than 5,000 yards in a career, putting together 5,883 yards total offense and topping Bob Briese's Purdue mark by some 1,000 yards. His three-year passing log read 375 of 733 for 5,423 yards and 37 touchdowns.

When the season ended he made almost all the major all-America teams and was named the Outstanding Player in College Football by *Sport* Magazine. The only minor disappointment was his second-place finish in the Heisman balloting to running back Steve Owens of Oklahoma.

Mike was also an Academic all-America once more and worked to get his degree. But he also began looking forward to the pro draft. He now felt he could do the job in the big time. And the people who had worked with him at Purdue had nothing but good things to say about the personable Phipps.

"Without Mike this year's team could have easily been 2-8 instead of 8-2," said Coach Mollenkopf. "I can't say how much he meant to us because the job he did was fantastic. You couldn't measure his value to this team. He didn't have 10 other all-Americans working with him, but he got all the kids to pull together and made us a big winner again."

Coach DeMoss, the quarterback mentor who was to take over as head coach after Mike left, had worked closely with the youngster for three years.

"Mike has the same qualities and talents that both Dawson and Griese had," DeMoss said. "They've both made it in the pros and Mike should make it the same way. He's bigger and stronger than either Len or Bob. And he has that great, quick release of the football. Plus we feel he has the knowledge of the game that will enable him to make smooth transition to the pros."

Even Mrs. Wilma Rickey, who served as secretary to the Purdue coaches, talked about what a fine young man Mike was.

"Mike is simply tops," Mrs. Rickey said, "a real gentleman of the first order. He's modest, sincere and humble—a very pleasant young man to be around. We would love to have him for another three years and a lot more like him."

But everyone, including Mike, knew his college days were behind him and he couldn't rest on past laurels. He had a bright future ahead of him, but one that would take hard work, long hours, and perhaps cause considerable pain.

"I had to work hard when I went from high school ball into college," said Mike. "There were new things to learn and another level of competition to get used to. The pros are another step forward and there's a great opportunity awaiting me if I get some breaks and work hard—and believe me, I'm certainly planning to work hard."

There was much speculation about which team would take Mike. Terry Bradshaw and Dennis Shaw were the two other high-ranking quarterbacks coming out of the college ranks and it was judged a tossup as to which one would go first. Mike was asked which team he would most like to play for.

"There's no way I can figure who's going to take me," he said, "so I'm kind of playing the whole thing by ear. "Pittsburgh picks first and the Bears second. I've spoken with some of the Chicago people and they said they'd like to have a shot at me. Of course, they may pick Bradshaw ahead of me, I don't know.

"If the Bears draft me they might give me a chance early. But I wouldn't really want to step into a starting role before I'm ready. I'd like to work into it, then earn it. When I go into a game I want to be ready and fully able to execute.

"I guess it's possible to play regular the first year but it isn't easy. Recognition of defenses is part of it. Pro defensive players are so much quicker that your passes must be more accurate and get there faster than in college. You've got to get into that pocket quickly and stay there. The whole business is a lot of work."

Mike, of course, wasn't aware of the behind-the-scenes shuffling that was taking place. The Cleveland Browns were at the point where Bill Nelsen's knees had become a very perishable commodity. Many considered them worse than Namath's. So the Browns cooked up the deal that sent Warfield to Miami in return for the number three draft choice. At the same time Green Bay made a deal with Chicago that gave the Packers the second pick. So the order was Pittsburgh, Green Bay, Cleveland, and it was a good guess that quarterbacks would be taken by two or possibly all three of the teams.

Many experts figured that Phipps was better prepared for the pros than Bradshaw because of the level of competition at college. One guy who thought so was Joe Thomas, the man who was in the process of molding the Dolphins and had Phipps' predecessor at Purdue, Bob Griese. Said Thomas:

"I think Phipps is the premier pro football prospect among the current college seniors, and that's taking in all the positions. He's 6-3, strong, has a great arm, and is a natural pro."

So the draft finally rolled around late in January of 1970. The Steelers had the first choice and surprised some by picking Bradshaw. They believed Terry had a better long-range future than Mike. Green Bay came next and took Mike McCoy, the huge tackle from Notre Dame. Then came Cleveland with the third pick and they took Phipps.

'I hope I'll be able to help the Browns right away," Mike said, after learning of his selection. "And I also hope I get the opportunity to play right away. I don't know Bill Nelsen but from his record with the Browns it looks as if he's a first class quarterback."

Mike had a friend from Evansville, Indiana, Ferris Traylor, help him with his negotiations. There were no major problems with Cleveland owner Art Modell, but it wasn't until early July that Mike finally signed. The deal was a big one, a five-year pact estimated to be in the neighborhood of $250,000. It was based on the fact that Mike would undergo a two- or three-year learning process. There were incentive clauses which covered the possibility of Mike playing full time sooner. Much of that depended on Nelsen's bad knees.

Before reporting to the Browns, Mike went to Chicago to play in the College All-star game against the world champion Kansas City Chiefs. Bradshaw had a slight injury and wasn't on the Stars' roster. Phipps and Dennis Shaw (drafted by Buffalo) were the quarterbacks.

Shaw got the starting call and couldn't move the team. K.C. opened by moving well against the inexperienced collegians and piled up a 17-0 lead before the second quarter began. That's when Coach Otto Graham made the switch to Phipps.

The All-Star offense was disorganized and overmatched in the opening session, but with Mike at the helm they drove past midfield three times in the second period against one of the toughest defenses in pro football. Mike didn't get his club on the scoreboard, but the observers from the pros were impressed. He hurt a shoulder early in the third period and since the Chiefs already had a 24-0 lead Coach Graham felt it best to keep him on the bench the rest of the way.

One of those who liked Mike was K.C. Coach Hank Stram. Said Stram, "Phipps is a sound quarterback with an excellent arm. We didn't expect a college man to read our defenses so well. If he had better help executing he could have put some points up against us."

When Mike reported to the Browns, the coaches began working with him fervishly, trying to make up for lost time and get him ready in case Nelsen's knees didn't hold up. Bill's knees were one of the sad stories in pro ball. Not yet 30 years old, the Browns signal-caller had had three knee operations. He was just coming into his own as one of the best in the game, yet knew that his days in the game he loved were numbered.

"I'm too occupied in a game to be worried about the knees," Nelsen said. "But I have a definite fear of hurting them more. I don't really want to go through a fourth operation. The knees ache all the time. I sometimes have trouble just walking on Monday and Tuesday after a game and after an hour and a half of practice.

"It's just faith in my line with their great blocking ability that keeps me in this thing. I always keep the knee wrapped, even off the field, except when I'm sleeping."

Nelsen was a limited quarterback when Mike joined the team. He was under strict orders not to run, no matter what, because the club figured that one play, one gain, even one win, wasn't worth the whole season.

Thus young Mike Phipps witnessed first hand the hazards of being a pro quarterback. It might have spooked many young players, but like most top athletes, Mike Phipps was willing to take great chances to compete in the big time. He and Nelsen became fast friends.

"I wish Mike the best," said Nelsen. "I hope he can help us whenever we need him. We've got fine coaches here and I can help him, as well. He has the physical ability and should be a good one.

"As far as I'm concerned he can have all the exhibition experience he wants. I know I'll be frothing at the bit to play, but I've got to change my ways. I can't play six exhibition games the way they play them now, which is as hard as in the regular season."

Strangely enough, the Browns didn't rush Phipps in

the exhibitions, in fact, they didn't play him much at all. Nelsen played more than he thought he would, and second-year man Don Gault also saw some action.

"Gault is slightly ahead of Phipps now," said Coach Skorich, "because of the previous exposure he's had with us. Mike got here after the All-Star game and had just three days before our first exhibition. It just worked out that he only played a few games. I think he threw five passes and completed two, and that's certainly not enough work.

"But when he was ready to play we were at the stage where we had to get our veterans ready. Quarterbacks must play to improve themselves and I guess we're in a little bit of a bind as far as that's concerned.

"Judging by practice sessions Mike is improving on schedule. He's throwing better and seems to be losing the hesitation he had earlier. He's also beginning to learn just how we use the passing game."

Nelsen was the Browns' quarterback when the season began and he led the club to an opening win over the New York Jets, 31-21. After a loss to San Francisco, the team whipped Pittsburgh and Cincinnati to get off to a good, 3-1, start. And despite the gimpy knees, the veteran was hanging in there for almost the entire game. Mike was a willing student on the sidelines, observing, handling the phones, talking to the coaches, and taking part in mid-game strategy sessions. Bradshaw was already a regular at Pittsburgh and Dennis Shaw had won the starting job at Buffalo. Phipps was the only one of the big three who wasn't seeing action. The reporters started asking about it.

"It doesn't bother me a bit," he said. "I've always said I'd be better off coming along slowly like this. I've got a great deal of confidence in the Cleveland coaching staff and I feel I'll get some experience the rest of the year."

Mike's first game action had come in the fourth-game win over Cleveland. He played briefly in the final quarter and said he wasn't nervous, but he was anxious to prove himself to his teammates and fans.

His next action came two weeks later when the club fell way behind Detroit and lost, 41-24. Mike played the second half of that one. He also got in for two series against Miami and one play against San Diego. It wasn't much, but as Mike said, every little bit helped.

The team was having a few problems finding the right balance on offense and defense. It seemed that the two units couldn't put things together the same week. But the club was still tied with Pittsburgh for the divisional lead, in spite of a mediocre 4-4 record. The next game was against the young Cincinnati Bengals, and early in the week Mike suddenly learned he was starting. Nelsen's knee was banged up and it was decided he should rest it a week.

"The news was a surprise to me," said Mike. "I've got some mixed emotions about it. I'm happy to be contributing but I know how badly Bill wants to play and how frustrating his knee problem is. We've become good friends and this kind of thing won't change anything."

In the first 18 minutes of the game it looked as if Mike was going to produce a storybook debut. He put 10 quick points on the board, driving the club downfield for a field goal, then tossing the first TD pass of his career. But the club couldn't keep up the momentum. The Bengal defense tightened and adjusted, some of Mike's receivers developed butter fingers.

The rest of the day was frustrating for the Browns. They couldn't score again. Cincy chipped away and crossed the goal line twice to eke out a 14-10 victory. Mike finished with 11 of 25 for 170 yards. Only one of his passes was intercepted. It wasn't great, but it wasn't bad, either.

"Mike did a good job," said Cleveland coach. "I thought five more passes should have been caught, but Mike can't throw and catch, too."

Nelsen returned the next week and finished out the season. It wasn't a good one for the Browns. The team was at 7-7 and out of the playoffs. As for Mike, his rookie log read 29 completions in 60 attempts for 529 yards, one touchdown, and five interceptions. He saw very little action.

Yet one longtime Cleveland sportswriter figured the job would be handed to Phipps during the 1971 camp and preseason because Nelsen's days were obviously numbered.

"Mike Phipps will be number one and much of the team's immediate future will be determined by where he can take it," the man wrote. But he later added, "Phipps is in the learning stage and it will take a while, and, even granting his talent, Phipps' future is as indeterminate as that of any gifted young quarterback."

As it turned out, the sportswriter was right. Before camp started Coach Skorich announced that Phipps would see the bulk of the action in the exhibitions and have a full chance to win the job. The implication was that the team was hoping Mike would win the job. It was just too risky to go with Nelsen much longer.

"I've never looked forward to a football season as I am to this one," Mike said, at the opening of camp. "I'm just tickled to be getting an opportunity, but I know I've got to prove I can do the job. The exhibitions will be a time of learning, but I also think it's important to win and go into the season with the right attitude."

But as the exhibitions started there was obvious disappointment in Mike's performance. He just wasn't improving fast enough. He seemed still to be hesitant and lacked the confidence needed to take charge. He just wasn't moving the team. There were two straight disasters, one against the Rams and the other versus the 49ers. But one thing Mike Phipps didn't do was make excuses. He told it like it was.

"The offense didn't move because of me," he said, flatly. "Mistakes killed us and I made most of them. It's not fun when you're making mistakes out there. I only hope I learn from them. Not scoring a point in an entire game is frustrating and I feel we let our defense down because they played so well.

"On the positive side is the fact that I've had more playing time and I can only expect to play better, a lot better. I knew it was going to be tough, but things always look so different out there than they do from the sidelines. My weaknesses are inexperience and forcing the ball."

The problem was that things didn't get better. People didn't want to admit it, but Mike Phipps wasn't doing the job and wasn't giving too many indications that he could. By the time the season started, Nelson was number one and Mike was back on the bench.

It was a bitter pill for the youngster to swallow, though he tried to accept the situation and make the most of it, he had to be aware of the mounting criticism against him. Paul Warfield was already showing his all-pro stuff at Miami. The original trade that gave the Browns the rights to draft Mike was dredged up again and again, second guessed, and chewed up. And the villain kept coming out Phipps.

To make matters worse for Mike, Nelsen showed immediately that he could still move the team that Mike stalled with. The club won four of its first five, fell off somewhat, but finished strong to enter the playoffs with a 9-5 record. Nelsen stayed in one piece throughout, and Mike saw even less action than he had as a rookie.

He was in long enough to throw the ball just 47 times, completing just 13 passes for a 27.7 percentage, and that's not even good enough for little league. He gained just 179 yards, threw for one TD with four intercepts. It was, in effect, an embarrassing performance.

In the first-round playoff game that year, the Browns fell to Baltimore, 20-3, and seemed out of it from the start. There was one play when Nelsen had the club on the six, dropped back to pass, had a clear road up the middle, yet he didn't run. He couldn't. Instead he threw an incomplete pass. It pointed up once again that Nelsen had no mobility left. Something had to be done. Even a Colt coach admitted his team took advantage of Bill's knees.

"We did things we couldn't do against another club because we knew Nelsen couldn't go anywhere. We took chances that would be too dangerous against a quarterback who could run."

What all this meant was that Coach Skorich and the Browns faced a big decision before the 1972 season. Would they give young Mike Phipps another shot? Or would they throw in the towel and begin searching again for a new quarterback?

"I would go with Phipps," one Cleveland newsman wrote. "Skorich should tell him, 'This is your team. You're the leader. Run the show.' And let him take it from there. If the Browns hope to go any further they'll need a healthy, young quarterback to do it."

For 1972, the Browns gave Phipps the quarterback job. It would be up to him to prove he could do it.

"Mike has all the qualities to be a great quarterback," Skorich said again. "He's as quick as anybody. He is a fine athlete with great speed, but he just hasn't played enough to get the feel of the pro game. The hardest thing for a young QB is to go to the right man at the right time. And there's no cure except experience. We hope to give Mike that in the pre-season."

The pressure on Mike was tremendous. It was already his third year, and the failure of 1971 weighed heavily on his shoulders.

In the early days of camp a player who didn't want to be named told a reporter that he didn't think the experiment would work. As he talked, he pointed to the veteran Nelsen and said:

"There's our quarterback. He can call the plays and get the job done. With Phipps in the huddle it's like a board of directors meeting trying to decided what to do. Nelsen is a winner. This team has to go with him."

Then came another exhibition disaster in Los Angeles, and people began writing Phipps off once again. He threw an early interception and that was it. His confidence blunted, he led the team to just a field goal in four quarters.

But against San Francisco the following week he began to come on. He kept one drive going with a daring, gutty run up the middle that gained 17 yards. That was the one thing Nelsen couldn't do no matter how badly he wanted to. The run showed some of the vets that the kid had desire after all.

His passing was better, more decisive, and although the team lost, 20-13, Mike had taken a giant step. He continued to progress, but not far enough that Skorich had real confidence in him. Veteran Nelsen agreed that Phipps should have the job if he could handle it. But when the opener with Green Bay rolled around, Coach Skorich turned to his veteran once more.

So Mike found himself on the sidelines again, watching Nelsen directing the team. It could have been a fatal blow to his spirits, but somehow Mike remained optimistic.

On the field something new was happening. Nelsen wasn't moving the team. Clarence Scott grabbed off a Green Bay pass and ran 55 yards to the end zone. In the second period a Dan Cockroft field goal gave the Browns a 10-7 lead. But then the Packers took over and Nelsen couldn't get the team back into it. He had two passes picked off and was obviously having more knee problems. Midway through the period Skorich realized what he had to do. He inserted Mike Phipps into the lineup.

Mike finished the game and although the Browns lost, 26-10, he played well enough to merit another chance. Skorich said he'd stay with the youngster the next week against the Eagles. It would be only his third pro start.

But it was an important one, for it signalled the beginning of a new quarterback era for the Browns. It's hard to say what happened. Maybe Mike figured it was no use coming on uptight. He just stayed loose and let the chips fall as they might.

The first fell in the form of a 22-yard touchdown pass to wide receiver Frank Pitts. Then there was another drive with fullback Bo Scott scoring on a short plunge. It was 20-3 at halftime, and when Mike ran four yards for another score in the third quarter it went to 27-3. The Eagles rallied but Cleveland held on for a 27-17 victory, Mike's first win in a starting role.

He hadn't done badly, connecting on nine of 20 passes for 152 yards and a TD. When it was over,

Mike just sighed. "It's about time," he said. And he was further rewarded when Coach Skorich quickly said that Mike would continue as the team's quarterback. The next game would be a tough one, against the always pesky Cincinnati Bengals.

The game turned out to be easier than expected, thanks to the alert play of the Cleveland defensive unit which picked off two passes and recovered a pair of Cincy fumbles. But it was also another step forward for Mike. He hit on 12 of 24 passes for 198 yards and began earning respect from friend and foe alike when he connected with Pitts on a beautiful 68-yard scoring strike.

Then came a bad game. It was bound to happen. Mike threw four intercepts as Kansas City whipped the Browns, 31-7. The next week it was even worse. Chicago shut out the Browns, 17-0. Mike was nine for 19, netting 126 yards, but the ground game broke down completely. The team was at 2-3 and seemingly ready to flounder. If Skorich was going to quit on Mike, this was the time. But he quickly announced that Phipps would remain at the helm.

The game with Houston was a turning point and began what was to be a series of heroics for Mike Phipps. The Browns fell behind early, but came back when Mike hit Pitts for a 27-yard TD. However, the Oilers took over again in the third period and led 17-16 midway through the fourth. A loss here would all but end any playoff hopes the Browns might have.

But Mike didn't panic. Midway through the period he led a drive that covered some 80 yards, mixing his plays well, passing with authority, and scrambling himself when he had to. He finally sneaked it over from the one and gave the browns a 23-17 win.

At Denver the following week Mike had to play on a windswept, snowy field. Once again it was a close game into the fourth quarter, and once again Mike Phipps led a final drive, covering 74 yards, and took it in himself for the winning score. He completed 15 of 33 passes for 178 yards in that one as the Browns won, 27-20.

An easy victory over Houston followed. Then came the crucial game with San Diego, the one in which Mike fired the 38-yard strike to Pitts with just 41 seconds left to snatch the game from the jaws of defeat. Now the veteran players who had always been Nelsen followers were beginning to believe that the youngster had what it took to run the club.

The game against Pittsburgh was another big one. Mike got the club a big lead, hitting Pitts from 17 yards out with a TD toss that made it 20-3 in the second quarter. But the Steelers came back and actually took a 24-23 lead into the final minutes.

So Mike went to work again with what was becoming the normal last-minute drive. This time he took the team from its own 42 to the Steeler 26, where Don Cockroft booted the winning field goal. The key play was a 16-yard keeper play which Mike improvised when he saw the Steelers keying for an end around which he had called. It was a clutch play and another big win.

"We've been winning and that's the big thing for me," Mike said, after hitting 14 of 25 for 194 yards against the Steelers. "I had to show the others I could run the team, could put points up, could get the job done. And it's been a difficult thing."

The final game of the season was against the New York Jets. The Browns already had a wild card berth in the playoffs but wanted a last victory for a 10-4 season. By now Mike was very comfortable in his new role. The game was close for awhile, but he and Pitts broke it up by combining on a perfect, 80-yard, pass-run touchdown play. Mike threw for 156 yards and ran for 38 more in this final game of the season.

"I know that any developing quarterback is going to make mistakes," Mike said, after that final game. "It's inevitable. But the important thing is to learn from them and not to repeat them. I think once I recognized this I was on my way to becoming a pro quarterback.

"I'm still learning my trade," he continued. "I know I'm not a complete pro yet. But I learned to do one important thing. I know now that I can come back from a mistake and still win. That kind of confidence is very necessary."

The other Browns also acknowledged Mike's new role as leader. Most of them said that he is basically a quiet guy, and that's why it took them longer to realize that he was coming on and taking charge. Some of them took the quietness as a lack of confidence, others as aloofness. When they realized it was just his way, the problem was solved. All those last-minute victories didn't hurt, either.

In his first full season Mike had thrown the ball 305 times, completing 144 for a 47.2 percentage and 1,994 yards. He threw for 13 touchdowns and had 16 passes intercepted. There was still room for improvement, but it was certainly a solid beginning. He was even happier when his teammates voted him and receiver Pitts as co-MVP's for the 1972 season.

But that season wasn't over yet. The Browns still had the playoffs and would face the amazing Miami Dolphins in round one. The Dolphins had just completed a perfect, 14-0-0, season and were heavy favorites to win it all.

The Dolphins scored early when Charley Babb blocked a Cockroft punt attempt and then took it five yards to the end zone. Shortly before the half Garo Yepremian kicked a 40-yard field goal and the Dolphins led 10-0. Mike and the offensive unit were having trouble with the great zone defense of the Dolphins.

But in the third quarter Mike led a controlled drive that resulted in a score when he ran it in himself from the five. And after another Yepremian field goal, Mike marched the team downfield again and this time hit flanker Fair Hooker with a 27-yard scoring strike. The Browns led 14-13 and smelled upset.

Only it didn't happen. Miami was a great clutch team, too, and they drove 80 yards in the closing minutes to score the winning touchdown. Cleveland had a last chance, but a hassled Phipps threw his fifth interception of the day and the Dolphins won, 20-14.

The game showed that Mike had come a long way, but still had more to come. Five intercepts is just too many, even against a crack defensive team like the Dolphins. Yet he had also led two clutch drives that had given his team the lead in the final period. And it was Mike's play, to a large degree, that got the

Browns to the playoffs in the first place. So there was definitely a future with Mr. Phipps.

Mike was looking forward to the 1973 season with increased eagerness.

"I hope to get up at least 50 percent in pass completions," he said, at the outset of training camp. "I want to bring down my interceptions. To me, an interception is like giving up some points. I also want to get at least a touchdown pass for every interception and would like to have more TD passes than intercepts.

"I think I'll have more responsibilities this season as far as running the game. I realize I still have limitations and won't mind any help I can get.

"It was a tough fight. You have to earn loyalty from your teammates. You have to show them you can win. Success brings friends and togetherness."

Mike's center for the latter part of '72 and also in '73 was Bob DeMarco, a great veteran who had played on several teams. He felt Mike had what it takes.

"Phipps has everything to be a really great quarterback," said DeMarco. "He can be better than Griese because he's bigger and stronger. I think he's also got a better arm and he can stay in the pocket longer; that helps.

"When he has to, Mike is also a strong runner and can scramble well. Heck, he ran for more than 250 yards last year. It's only a matter of time now, experience, confidence, the things he'll be picking up as we go along. There were some times last year when he was a bit hesitant, but he should lose that."

Unfortunately, Mike was coming of age when some of the other Browns were going downhill. The great Leroy Kelly, the speedy halfback who had been a great runner for a decade, was finally slowing down. He gained 811 yards in '72, but was plagued by injuries most of 1973 and held to 389 yards. Fullback Bo Scott was also hurt most of the year. That meant that the Cleveland ground game, feared since the advent of Jim Brown in 1957, came to an abrupt halt, putting more pressure on Phipps.

There was also the lack of a big receiver. Pitts was over 30 and starting to show it. He wasn't as effective as he had been in '72. So the offense was in trouble. The defense was good, but not great. The club still had the ability to win, but not excel. The season turned into a mediocre 7-5-2 campaign with no playoff position.

There were some good wins over Oakland, Pittsburgh, Kansas City, and a close loss to champion Miami. But the crusher came in the final two games when the Browns didn't have enough left, losing to Cincinnati, 34-17, and L.A., 30-17. If they could have won those two, it would have been another playoff year. So it was still pretty close.

Mike was the only quarterback now. Nelsen retired and was coaching Jim Plunkett at New England. So Mike played all the way. Understudy Don Horn threw just eight passes.

It was another learning year. The problems with the running game and receivers didn't help Mike and he fell short of some of his goals. He fired 299 passes and completed 148, just under 50 percent. His yardage was down to 1,719, indicating the lack of a deep threat. He threw for just nine TDs and had 20 passes picked off. Again, he was playing catch-up very often and had to gamble, especially when the defenders knew he didn't have a running game to call upon.

So Mike had a rough year. In fact, his pro career hasn't been easy. There were the two years on the bench, the struggle to win a job, now the decline of the team. Of course, the Browns have a rich winning tradition behind them. They've always been able to regroup faster than most. Perhaps it will happen again.

If it doesn't, if the team continues to go downhill, times will be hard once again for Mike Phipps. As everyone has said, he's got all the tools. And in 1972 he was starting to get the confidence. Now he needs the players to complete the picture. It used to be that the Browns wondered if they had a quarterback to go with the team. Now they've got to wonder if they have a team to go with the quarterback.

For Mike Phipps is a good one, and he's got the potential to be even better. He's on the right road now. The future seems to be his.

STATISTICS

Billy Kilmer

Team	Year	Att.	Comp.	Pct.	Yds.	TD	Int.	Ave. Gain
San Francisco	1961	34	19	.559	286	0	4	8.41
San Francisco	1962	13	8	.615	191	1	3	14.69
San Francisco	1963			did not play				
San Francisco	1964	14	8	.571	92	1	1	6.57
San Francisco	1965			did not play				
San Francisco	1966	16	5	.313	84	0	1	5.25
New Orleans	1967	204	97	.475	1,341	6	11	6.57
New Orleans	1968	315	167	.530	2,060	15	17	6.54
New Orleans	1969	360	193	.536	2,532	20	17	7.03
New Orleans	1970	237	135	.570	1,557	6	17	6.57
Washington	1971	306	166	.542	2,221	13	13	7.26
Washington	1972	225	120	.533	1,648	19	11	7.32
Washington	1973	227	122	.537	1,656	14	9	7.29
Pro Totals		1,951	1,040	.533	13,668	95	104	7.00

Terry Bradshaw

Team	Year	Att.	Comp.	Pct.	Yds.	TD	Int.	Ave. Gain
Pittsburgh	1970	218	83	.381	1,410	6	24	6.47
Pittsburgh	1971	373	203	.544	2,259	13	22	6.05
Pittsburgh	1972	308	147	.477	1,887	12	12	6.13
Pittsburgh	1973	180	89	.494	1,183	10	15	6.57
Pro Totals		1,079	522	.484	6,739	41	73	6.24

John Hadl

Team	Year	Att.	Comp.	Pct.	Yds.	TD	Int.	Ave. Gain
San Diego	1962	260	107	.411	1,632	15	24	6.28
San Diego	1963	64	28	.438	502	6	6	7.84
San Diego	1964	274	147	.536	2,157	18	15	7.87
San Diego	1965	348	174	.500	2,798	20	21	8.04
San Diego	1966	375	200	.533	2,846	23	14	7.59
San Diego	1967	427	217	.508	3,365	24	22	7.88
San Diego	1968	440	208	.473	3,473	27	32	7.89
San Diego	1969	324	158	.488	2,253	10	11	6.95
San Diego	1970	327	162	.495	2,388	22	15	7.30
San Diego	1971	431	233	.541	3,075	21	25	7.13
San Diego	1972	370	190	.514	2,449	15	26	6.62
Los Angeles	1973	258	135	.523	2,008	22	11	7.78
Pro Totals		3,899	1,959	.502	28,946	223	222	7.42

Mike Phipps

Team	Year	Att.	Comp.	Pct.	Yds.	TD	Int.	Ave. Gain
Cleveland	1970	60	29	.483	529	1	5	8.82
Cleveland	1971	47	13	.277	179	1	4	3.81
Cleveland	1972	305	144	.472	1,994	13	16	6.54
Cleveland	1973	299	148	.495	1,719	9	20	5.75
Pro Totals		711	334	.470	4,421	24	45	6.22